Praise for *We Do This 'Til We Free Us*

"This book writes a political genealogy of one of our movement era's most significant intellectuals and community organizers and her people into the record of a feminist and abolitionist Black Radical Tradition. She teaches us to praise the choir, appreciate vulnerability, and be disciplined in service of transforming ourselves and the world in which we live." —CHARLENE A. CARRUTHERS, author, *Unapologetic: A Black, Queer, and Feminist Mandate for Radical Movements*

"Mariame Kaba isn't trying to save the world. Instead, this collection of liberatory practice serves as a building block for a new kind of existence, filled with the hum only evolved humanity can sound. Kaba returns questions unanswered; Kaba spirits the flame untethered; Kaba is the water well in the middle of a thirsty town. And in her unyielding abolition work, Mariame Kaba reveals our reflection's purpose. She is generous in offering us a blueprint to save ourselves." —MAHOGANY L. BROWNE, author, *Chlorine Sky*

"So many of us have been introduced to abolition—or invited into a deeper understanding and practice of abolitionist politics—through Mariame Kaba's words, work, and vision, as well as her brilliant sense of humor, skillful use of Twitter, love of poetry, practice of hope, and appreciation of art. For those of us new to abolition, this book is the primer we need. For those of us who have been on an abolitionist journey, it is full of the reminders we need. No matter where and how you enter the conversation, *We Do This 'Til We Free Us* brings all of us infinitely closer to creating a world premised on genuine and lasting safety, justice, and peace." —ANDREA J. RITCHIE, author, *Invisible No More: Police Violence against Black Women and Women of Color*

"Anyone and everyone who has had the privilege of learning from Mariame Kaba has been transformed into a better thinker, organizer, artist, and human. What Kaba does is light the path to abolition and liberation with equal parts intelligence and compassion, experience and hope. This book brings together the scattered pieces of her wisdom she has shared publicly in different venues so that those who don't have the pleasure of sitting and learning with her can absorb a small part of what makes Kaba one of the most impressive and important thinkers and organizers of our time. Let this work fortify those who are already engaged in the struggle and be an energetic spark for those just starting out on this path to freedom." —MYCHAL DENZEL SMITH, author, *Stakes Is High: Life after the American Dream*

"Mariame has the rarest of gifts: the ability to imagine a better future, the skills to help construct it, and the courage to demand it. For years, Mariame has been thinking through some of the toughest questions about society's addiction to punishment, and We Do This 'Til We Free Us showcases the extraordinary depths of her knowledge about our criminal legal system. This book could not arrive at a better time—as more people become familiar with abolition, Mariame's words are especially critical. But it is not just a book about systems. It's a book about people, the powerful and the struggling. And, ultimately it is a book about each of us—the values we possess and the choices we make. Mariame has the uncanny ability to illuminate the murky and complicated elements of who we are and give them voice. As an abolitionist, Mariame is not just calling for the destruction of old systems but also the creation of a new world. This book will change the way you think about your community, your relationships, and yourself." —JOSIE DUFFY RICE, writer

"Mariame Kaba is a people's historian, an ultra-practical problem solver, and a visionary prophet whose work dreams and builds a world made by collaboration and healing where putting people in cages is unimaginable. We Do This 'Til We Free Us is packed with Kaba's brilliant insights and detailed examples of how the work of abolition is put into practice in grassroots campaigns. Kaba's boundless creativity is rooted in her rigorous study of resistance and inspiration, and the wisdom of her words is woven through with poetry, literature, history, and music, so that her offerings are both grounded in practical discernment and inclined toward our most robust imagination of what freedom could mean. This book will be both a practical tool and a source of comfort in hard times for change-makers and world-builders." —DEAN SPADE, author, Mutual Aid: Building Solidarity During This Crisis (and the Next)

"This suite of essays and interviews blends the verve, insight, skill, and generosity of one of the most brilliant abolitionist thinkers, curators, and organizers of our time. Marked by lush imagination, care, and strategic acumen, We Do This 'Til We Free Us is a manual for all those who want to create new collectivities and new futures from the ashes of entire systems of carcerality, racism, sexism, and capitalism. Always teaching us how to 'have each other,' there is no wiser or more inspirational figure in the fight for justice than Mariame Kaba." —SARAH HALEY, author, No Mercy Here: Gender, Punishment, and the Making of Jim Crow Modernity

"We Do This 'Til We Free Us is an organizer's gift: a vision of abolition that is also a practice of it and a road map. Essay by essay, Mariame Kaba guides us through the abolitionist futures she has created in real time by turning

questions into experiments, learning from failures as much as successes, and doing everything with other people. Let her words radicalize you, let them unlock your imagination, let them teach you how to practice hope, and let them show you why the everyday is the terrain of our greatest abolitionist creations. *We Do This 'Til We Free Us* is not a book to be read; it is a portal to a collective project of liberation that literally requires every last one of us."
—**LAURA McTIGHE, Front Porch Research Strategies and assistant professor, Florida State University**

"In her new book, *We Do This 'Til We Free Us* Mariame Kaba demonstrates the ways that discipline—in intellect, in practice, in relationship—leads not to despair, but to hope. The far-ranging series of essays and interviews draws on her deep practice as a seasoned organizer who persistently distills the questions surrounding abolition to basic human decisions about the world we want to inhabit and how we will go about building it. Abolition, as Mariame sees and practices, is fundamentally both generous, and pragmatic and her writing will move both seasoned abolitionists and those just now asking these questions for the first time to join in her conclusion that 'your cynicism is unrealistic.'" —**DANIELLE SERED, author, *Until We Reckon: Violence, Mass Incarceration, and a Road to Repair***

"Mariame's wisdom trues my restorative justice compass. The restorative justice movement has much to learn from Mariame's steadfast commitment to protecting our approaches to harm and healing from state co-optation and control. Her unwavering belief in 'we got us' offers powerful inspiration to imagine, ground, and elevate our practice. What a gift!" —**SUJATHA BALIGA, restorative justice practitioner**

"The intertwined analysis and collective organizing archived in this invaluable collection provides crucial entry points in the everyday work of abolition. Engaging the most pressing questions of our time with clarity and commitment, as always, Mariame makes abolition irresistible and, as imperatively, doable." —**ERICA R. MEINERS, author, *For the Children: Protecting Innocence in a Carceral State***

"Working through a range of concepts and struggles—from the criminalization of self-defense to what is needed to inspire our imaginations toward abolition— *We Do This 'Til We Free Us* truly demonstrates, Mariame Kaba's teachings that 'hope is a discipline.' With this book Kaba brings with her a community of organizers, workers, and writers to show us how abolition is a practice and to guide our actions for liberation." —**SIMONE BROWNE, author, *Dark Matters: On the Surveillance of Blackness***

"For the last twenty-five years, prison abolitionists have been treated like the Don Quixotes of social justice movements, chasing an impossibly unrealistic vision. In *We Do This 'Til We Free Us*, Kaba demonstrates, through her work as an organizer and scholar, that putting an end to the carceral state is not only necessary but also possible. This collection offers a remarkable history of abolitionist organizing and a road map for the work we must do to make a new world and transform ourselves in the process." —**KENYON FARROW, Co-Executive Director, Partners for Dignity & Rights**

"*We Do This 'Til We Free Us* is a beacon, a watch fire, a guidepost for all of us who are seeking transformational and life-giving change in a death-dealing society. Mariame Kaba is a force of nature, unafraid to step into great storms of violence. As this long-awaited collection of abolitionist essays, interviews, and conversations demonstrates, Kaba knows that relationships are at the center of everything; that new possibilities and insights arise from the organized efforts of ordinary people; that only collective endeavor can move us forward. This isn't simply a book. It's a portal." —**KAY WHITLOCK, coauthor *Queer (In) Justice: The Criminalization of LGBT People in the United States***

"Mariame Kaba's *We Do This 'Til We Free Us* exudes her brilliance as an organizer, educator, and visionary. A primer in abolition as an organizing vision, strategy, and practice, this collection of essays is rooted in a structural analysis of policing, incarceration, and surveillance while uplifting collective strategies, actions, and practices that lend themselves toward ending these systems. The collection shares some of the amazing abolitionist projects she's initiated, organized, and nurtured, and is a testament to the power of collectivity and community. This is a book for those who have never thought about abolition and for those who have thought about it for years. Through the lens Mariame Kaba offers, the possibilities for abolition become quite tangible, possible, even inevitable." —**ANN RUSSO, author, *Feminist Accountability: Disrupting Violence and Transforming Power***

"If ever there was a time we needed Mariame Kaba's words and insights all in one place, it is now! Principled, pragmatic, and, most of all, visionary, *We Do This 'Til We Free Us* not only casts an unflinching light on our violent carceral system but also illuminates real pathways towards justice and freedom. This book should be read, studied, and acted upon by everyone committed to seeding new worlds amidst the ruins of the old." —**RUHA BENJAMIN, Princeton University**

"*We Do This 'Til We Free Us* is a series of essays that operate as gifts, reflections, and political interventions from the humbly prolific organizer Mariame

Kaba. Whether contending with abolitionist organizing, the application of transformative justice, or relationships as survival, she creates necessary guideposts for all of us. This is a deliciously nuanced read, one that you will pick up multiple times and receive something new each time. And this is a book designed to accompany your political endeavors, inspiring you to deepen your activism and organizing, and insisting that you, alongside Mariame, have a place in the creation of a more liberatory society." —EJERIS DIXON, **organizer, strategist, facilitator, and coeditor of Beyond Survival: Stories and Strategies of the Transformative Justice Movement**

"Brimming with organizing insights and burning questions, this collection is a must-read for those engaged in, or looking to learn more about the movement to abolish the prison-industrial complex. We Do This 'Til We Free Us so clearly and beautifully shows us that the road to abolition is paved in collective struggle, solidarity, accountability, love, and 'a million different little experiments.'" —EMILY THUMA, **author, All Our Trials: Prisons, Policing, and the Feminist Fight to End Violence**

"This long-awaited collection of the works of Mariame Kaba is what the movement for abolition needs right now. Kaba blends radical critique, historical analysis, ground theory, and practical application to help guide organizers building an abolitionist future. There are very few scholars and/ or organizers who are able to seamlessly bring abolitionist and transformative justice theory with practical organizing strategies as Kaba so successfully does. Kaba's essays also demonstrate the transformation our movements need to make so that they are guided by principles of love and care that can sustain our communities into a different world. She teaches how to build the discipline necessary so that we can be guided by hope rather than despair. Kaba's work is a true gift to the movement." —ANDREA SMITH, **professor of ethnic studies, University of California, Riverside**

"Mariame Kaba is a political genius and truth-teller for our times, as an abolitionist, political organizer, educator, and writer, she is audacious in her dreams for our Black future freedoms. This book says what needs to be said in this political moment as we reckon with abolition in response to police brutality, white supremacy, and a pandemic that is disproportionately killing people of color globally. Each chapter is a beautiful and archival testimonial to the lineage of Black organizing, especially Black feminists, that have led us to this political and cultural moment of mass uprisings creating resilient, abolitionist, and transformative strategies in the face of police brutality, massive incarceration, and the genocidal state response to COVID19. We Do

This 'Til We Free Us is a remedy for our collective survival, and a manifesto for responding to harms and violence for our future." —**CARA PAGE, founder of Changing Frequencies**

"Mariame Kaba's *We Do This 'Til We Free Us* is a treasure trove of essays and interviews that shares her knowledge, insights, and wisdom developed over decades of organizing against the prison industrial complex and supporting survivors of violence. In this book, Kaba recounts scores of campaigns, projects, collaborations, and activists that brought us to historic moments in 2020 and beyond, and provides concrete steps people can take on the path to abolition. A brilliant organizer, educator, political theorist, and preeminent abolitionist of the twenty-first century, Kaba succinctly breaks down the anti-Black foundations of the US criminal legal system and makes the case for abolition and transformative justice. This book is a must read for anyone striving for more peace and justice in this world." —**JOEY MOGUL, coauthor, *Queer (In)Justice: The Criminalization of LGBT People in the United States***

"This collection of writings embodies Mariame's gifts to the abolitionist movement, not only in content but in format. As readers, we are invited into the conversations Kaba has been having for decades as she lifts up countless stories that belong to the larger movement of which she is an essential leader. We are offered Mariame's personal and also collaborative writing that highlights a central message running throughout the book; we will not achieve liberation alone. While there are no blueprints for abolition, this text is a guiding light that offers crucial answers and an expansive invitation for all to join in the work." —**REV. JASON LYDON, Second Unitarian Church of Chicago**

"*We Do This 'Til We Free Us* outlines an approach to transformative politics that we have been hungry for: brilliant strategies that are at once practical and prophetic. For decades, Mariame Kaba's pathbreaking leadership has steered us towards a horizon of radical freedom that, as she has repeatedly demonstrated, is *within our reach*. This remarkable collection is a powerful map for anyone who longs for a future built on safety, community, and joy, and an intellectual home for those who are creating new pathways to get us there."— **ALISA BIERRIA, cofounder and co-organizer of Survived and Punished**

"Mariame Kaba's living example continuously teaches me that accountability and abolition are daily internal and external practices. *We Do This 'Til We Free Us* is both timely and timeless. This compelling collection is an offering of Kaba's thoughtful experiential perspectives and insights about the strenuous, compassionate, and rewarding work to not harm in response to witnessing and/ or experiencing harm. Kaba's words are a sacred road map for an embodied praxis that invites all of us to imagine, envision, and work collectively to co-create a society without violence." —**AISHAH SHAHIDAH SIMMONS, creator, NO! The Rape Documentary and author, Love WITH Accountability**

"We Do This 'Til We Free Us has so much wisdom to offer, particularly at this unprecedented moment. Kaba not only challenges the corrosive notions that only policing and prisons keep us safe but also invites us to see abolition not as a faraway goal but an everyday adventure that we can embark upon in our daily lives. Mariame Kaba is a galactic treasure. Her passion, dedication, and commitment to abolition, safety, and accountability are unparalleled. Read this book." —**VICTORIA LAW, author, *Prison by Any Other Name***

"Mariame Kaba is one of the foremost grassroots intellectuals of our time. She is a strategic, brilliant, and practical genius whose intellectual and on-the-ground-work is foundational to the past twenty years of transformative justice and abolitionist theory and practice. She's someone whose work I urge anyone to read who is curious about exactly why and how we are going to dismantle prisons and build the different future we need. I am so happy to have this book in the world, collecting so many of my favorite pieces, to give to new and old comrades alike." —**LEAH LAKSHMI PIEPZNA-SAMARASINHA, author, *Care Work: Dreaming Disability Justice***

"The miracle is Mariame's collaborative, accountable, future-facing, legacy-bearing presence in our movements and her intentional practice of evaluating how she can contribute to our collective future. This book, which documents some of Kaba's most important interventions, crucial conversations and paradigm shifting ideas makes this ongoing miracle shareable, teachable, and available for study in community. We Do This 'Til We Free Us is a necessary offering towards the possibility of our intentional participation in the actions that will create a more loving and liveable world. Read this book, hold this archive, share this journey, to nurture your own presence, practice and collaborations towards the freedom we already deserve." —**ALEXIS PAULINE GUMBS, author, *Dub: Finding Ceremony***

"Beautiful and timely, We Do This 'Til We Free Us is more than a book. It is a gathering: a conversation, a coming together, a call to be not only our best selves but also together in struggle. It is a how-to gift for all who believe in freedom from violence. In a wide-ranging series of essays, interviews, and speeches, inveterate organizer Mariame Kaba shares strategic wisdom from the abolitionist front lines. Read it, pass it on, and get to work!" —**DAN BERGER, author, *Rethinking the American Prison Movement***

The Abolitionist Papers Series
Edited by Naomi Murakawa

Also in this series:

Change Everything: Racial Capitalism and the Case for Abolition
Ruth Wilson Gilmore

Abolition. Feminism. Now.
Angela Y. Davis, Gina Dent, Beth Richie, and Erica Meiners

WE DO THIS 'TIL WE FREE US

ABOLITIONIST ORGANIZING AND TRANSFORMING JUSTICE

Mariame Kaba

Foreword by Naomi Murakawa

Edited by Tamara K. Nopper

Haymarket Books
Chicago, Illinois

Published in 2021 by
Haymarket Books
P.O. Box 180165
Chicago, IL 60618
773-583-7884
www.haymarketbooks.org
info@haymarketbooks.org

ISBN: 978-1-64259-525-3

Distributed to the trade in the US through Consortium Book Sales and Distribution (www.cbsd.com) and internationally through Ingram Publisher Services International (www.ingramcontent.com).

This book was published with the generous support of Lannan Foundation and Wallace Action Fund.

Special discounts are available for bulk purchases by organizations and institutions. Please email info@haymarketbooks.org for more information.

Cover artwork by Monica Trinidad.
Cover design by Eric Kerl.

Library of Congress Cataloging-in-Publication data is available.

10 9 8 7 6 5 4 3 2

To my father, Moussa Kaba, who taught me
that failures are always lessons and that
everything worthwhile is done with others

Contents

Foreword

Naomi Murakawa

January 2021

When Donald Trump incited his supporters to sack the US Capitol on January 6, 2021, the world saw rioters overtake the citadel of global power. With on-duty police taking selfies and off-duty police among the rioters, the insurrectionists easily breached the security perimeter and broke into the Capitol building, waving the Confederate flag and wearing neo-Nazi T-shirts. Shocked commentators wondered: How is it possible that a nation that spends $1 Trillion a year on security—military, police, and prisons, domestic and global surveillance—met thousands of white-supremacist rioters with a police response that ranged from the casually ill-prepared to the openly welcoming?

The question is misguided. White supremacy does not thrive in spite of the menacing infrastructure of US criminalization and militarism—it thrives because of it. The anti-Blackness of policing is not necessarily a point of shame but just a simple fact, an expectation summed up in the indignation of one pro-Trump rioter: "They're supposed to shoot BLM [Black Lives Matter], but they're shooting the patriots."

Police push millions of people into the criminal punishment system, where anti-Black death-dealing rises through each circle of hell. Black people comprise 13 percent of the US population but roughly 30 percent of the arrested, 35 percent of the imprisoned, 42 percent of those on death row, and 56 percent of those serving life sentences. Inside the largest prison system on the planet, the Covid-19 death rate is five times that of the general population. The roughly eight hundred US military bases the world over—like the nation's birth in native dispossession and slavery—reinforce the lessons that Trump's band of white brothers know all too well: take by force and invent the racial enemy. We live in the age of human sacrifice, says Ruth Wilson Gilmore, and our prison and military machinery normalizes industrialized killing.

We must abolish the prison-industrial complex—this is the opening premise of the Haymarket Books series the Abolitionist Papers. Beyond all that we must dismantle, abolition is a vision for all that we must build—and this makes it wonderfully fitting to inaugurate the series with the inspiring abolitionist builder Mariame Kaba.

Kaba's abolitionist vision burns so bright precisely because she refuses to be the single star, dazzling alone. Why be a star when you can make a constellation? And that's what we see in this book—the brilliance that shines from Kaba and an entire constellation of co-organizers, cofounders, and coconspirators, together in an abolitionist practice of refusal, care, and collectivity. Refusal: because we cannot collaborate with the prison-industrial complex, as "only evil will collaborate with evil" (June Jordan). Care: because "care is the antidote to violence" (Saidiya Hartman). Collectivity: because "everything worthwhile is done with others" (Moussa Kaba).

In Kaba's words, abolition envisions a world where we address harm without relying on the violent systems that increase it, a world where "we have everything we need: food, shelter, education, health, art, beauty, clean water, and more things that are foundational to our personal and community safety." Critics charge that abolitionists are naive about violence. But Kaba demonstrates that abolitionist analysis witnesses connections through every layer of violence—interpersonal violence, the state violence of criminalization and incarceration, and everywhere the structuring violence of anti-Blackness, heteropatriarchy, and capitalism.

Complex structures of violence become disturbingly clear when we center Black women and girls, as Kaba encourages us to do. For Bresha Meadows, Marissa Alexander, and thousands of Black women and girls who survived domestic and sexual violence by defending themselves, the criminal punishment system brings no relief, only more violence. Rather than neutralizing or countering interpersonal violence, state violence enables and reinforces the same oppression of racialized gender terror. After reading Kaba's analysis, it is clear that the criminal punishment system, not abolition, depends on a superficial view of violence, a facile view of good and evil based on the victim-perpetrator binary. Simple stories of the perfect victim and the monstrous perpetrator bend reality to fit the pretexts for state violence, helping us to pretend that the physical, emotional, social, and civic injuries of prison are somehow justice.

To readers who finish this book saying, "Yes, I understand, but now what?" Kaba's work is a portal connecting us to living currents of abolitionist organizing. If you nod in agreement while reading "Yes, We Literally Mean Abolish the Police," then let that spark lead you to the #DefundPolice Toolkit, created by Kaba, Woods Ervin, and Andrea Ritchie.* If you are a youth organizer, teacher, or parent, Kaba and collaborators have created *Defund Police: An Animated Video* with a companion discussion guide.† After reading "Free Us All: Participatory Defense Campaigns as Abolitionist Organizing," consider hosting a letter-writing event to support criminalized survivors.‡

Kaba has created and curated essential toolkits, artwork, and resource lists, but I highlight them not as magic formulas or shortcuts. There are no life hacks to revolution. As Robin D. G. Kelley reminds us, "Making a revolution is not a series of clever maneuvers and tactics, but a process that can and must transform us." Abolition requires dismantling the oppressive systems that live out there—and within us. Police not only protect private property and saturate Black, brown, and working-class neighborhoods. They also station themselves in our hearts and minds. Joining an organization, educating yourself about the prison-industrial complex, donating to a criminalized survivor's defense campaign: these are seemingly small doings to begin a process that can transform us. As Kaba tells us, start where you are. Connect with others already doing the work. Experiment.

This book gives us glimpses of Kaba becoming abolitionist, cultivating ways to reduce violence, to hold pain, to support and care.

* *#DefundPolice: Concrete Steps Toward Divestment from Policing and Investment in Community Safety*, created by Interrupting Criminalization: Research in Action (see interruptingcriminalization.com).
† *Defund Police: An Animated Video*, script by Mallory Hanora and Mariame Kaba, created by Project Nia and Blue Seat Studios (see project-nia.org).
‡ *Ideas and Tips for Organizing Letterwriting Events* (see survivedandpunished.org).

Becoming is a funny word, Imani Perry observes, because it means beautiful and a process of change. Not just a vision to behold, but a *doing* to arrive at a new state of being.

When asked what exactly a world without police and prisons would look like, Kaba returns the question to us, saying, "We'll figure it out by working to get there." Instead of certainty, she gives us as invitation to our future world—one where everyone has their needs met, where Black women are free, and therefore everyone is free, and where human disposability is unimaginable.

Mariame Kaba shows us that abolition is becoming. It is beautiful. And it is what we do 'til we free us.

Editor's Introduction

Tamara K. Nopper

December 2020

If you follow Mariame Kaba on social media, or even know a little bit about her resolute political work, it probably will not surprise you to learn that she was initially reticent about this book. Characteristically, Mariame wasn't sure an entire project should be solely developed around her. Over the years, Mariame has declined previous requests from Haymarket Books to publish a collection of her writings. As summer 2020 approached, Haymarket asked again.

As someone committed to building things, Mariame already had numerous projects lined up for the summer. From her home base in New York City, Mariame was running Project Nia, the organization she founded in 2009 to "end the arrest, detention, and incarceration of children and young adults by promoting restorative and transformative justice practices." She was also working with Andrea Ritchie and Woods Ervin on Interrupting Criminalization, an initiative of the Barnard Center for Research on Women's Social Justice Institute, which she cofounded with Ritchie in 2018. Along with running organizations, Mariame is always building or co-building campaigns.

Mariame was also managing increased requests for her time from the mainstream media. No doubt some of these inquiries directed her way stemmed from the growing public debate during the spring and summer of 2020 about defunding the police and abolition circulating on social media, in mainstream publications like *Good Housekeeping*, and on shows like *Good Morning America*. While the contemporary abolitionist movement is decades old, calls to defund the police rapidly gained traction in the United States during the first wave of the

Covid-19 pandemic. As public health expert Kenyon Farrow has noted, the US federal government's mendacious response to the Covid-19 crisis is nothing short of genocide.

In the midst of quarantine life and a deepening socioeconomic and emotional depression gripping the nation, many in the United States—and all over the world—courageously put their lives on the line and took to the streets to express their rage and sorrow at the murders of George Floyd and Breonna Taylor by police officers, and the hunting and murder of Ahmaud Arbery by white vigilantes. Protests occurred in cities all across the United States. In many cities cop cars were burned or flipped over, buildings set on fire, windows smashed, and stores looted. And in Minneapolis, where Floyd was killed by Derek Chauvin while other officers watched, a police precinct was torched. Some elected officials sought to quell the insurgency with symbolic gestures, such as painting the phrase "Black Lives Matter" on streets.

While satisfactory to some, many organizers and protesters made it clear that symbolism is not enough. They resisted such overtures in many ways, echoing the sentiment of Black freedom movement organizer Fannie Lou Hamer: "I'm sick of symbolic things. We are fighting for our lives."

As calls for defunding the police accelerated, so did broader conversations about abolition. When a publication date for *We Do This 'Til We Free Us* was announced on social media, numerous people responded immediately and enthusiastically, noting Mariame's power and influence as a political educator, and her direct impact on their thinking and activism. Many people have been waiting for this type of book from Mariame for a long time, and for good reason.

Hopefully, though, many readers will come to this book with no clue who Mariame Kaba is, or with little knowledge of her significance to the contemporary abolitionist movement. Simply, we want as many people as possible to learn more about abolition, and Mariame's writings and interviews provide a compelling introduction.

Mariame helps us make sense of how criminalization, regardless of race or class, is grounded in anti-Blackness. As she emphasizes in "A People's History of Prisons in the United States," included here, "You can't talk about criminalization in this country without understanding the history of Blackness and Black people in this country. Politicians have used us as the fuel to make things happen. We're always the canaries in the coal mine." In her discussions of #MeToo and #SayHerName, Mariame draws from her decades of organizing against gendered and sexual violence to raise provocative questions about supporting survivors and demands for accountability. Several pieces in *We Do This 'Til We Free Us* address how calls for carceral protection are used to criminalize women and girls, particularly those who are Black, engaging in self-defense, and detail Mariame's organizing in support of criminalized survivors. Mariame underscores why centralizing Black women's experiences with the criminal punishment system is urgent and necessary. This centering allows us to create conditions that support Black women's safety and well-being, and it sharpens our understanding of state violence. Mariame also encourages us to distinguish between policing and safety, and to build a society where people experience real safety in terms of the climate, the economy, our schools, our neighborhoods, our housing, and with each other.

This book also has constructive criticism for seasoned critics of the carceral state, including those who identify as abolitionists. Mariame's analysis is particularly relevant and instructive to those wishing to determine what accountability for harm and violence might look like if guided by abolitionist principles and values. As Mariame notes, "A big part of my life's work has been to try to imagine new ways of trying to address accountability and get accountability for survivors of violence." Addressing how "restorative justice" and "transformative justice" are often treated as interchangeable, Mariame observes how restorative justice initiatives are increasingly institutionalized in ways that differ from transformative justice.

Mariame also shares that she is grappling more with punishment and revenge as elements of carceral logic, even when enacted outside of the criminal legal system. One of Mariame's "touchstones," Angela Y. Davis, has said,

> We know, for example, that we replicate the structures of retributive punishment in our own relations to one another . . . even those of us who are conscious of that are still subject to that ideological influence on our emotional life. The retributive impulses of the state, the

retributive impulses of state punishment, are inscribed in our very individual emotional responses.

A critical examination of revenge is particularly useful and needed—including for readers who self-identify and organize as abolitionists. For example, in the interview "From 'Me Too' to 'All of Us': Organizing to End Sexual Violence without Prisons," included in this book, Mariame raises some very provocative points regarding the space politically available for grappling with tough and uncomfortable questions regarding supporting survivors. And in "Transforming Punishment: What Is Accountability without Punishment?" an essay about R. Kelly published for the first time here, Mariame and coauthor and Critical Resistance cofounder Rachel Herzing examine how the legal system deals with high-profile perpetrators of violence, as well as the public's thirst for punishment. As Mariame and Rachel underscore, this drive for retribution is sometimes expressed by those who claim to be abolitionists, yet this urge goes against abolition, and conflates individual emotional responses with political outcomes. As they state, "Abolitionism is not a politics mediated by emotional responses. Or, as we initially wanted to title this piece, abolition is not about your fucking feelings."

This book reveals Mariame to be a voracious reader, active listener, and courageous experimenter, and someone invested in serious thinking about her political work. Mariame also describes shifts in her thinking and approach. For example, Mariame shares how, as a teenager living in New York City, she came to abolitionist work via the police murders of Black men and boys—in the process, she did not always foreground gender justice. Mariame discusses how she learned to situate herself as a Black woman in her analysis, and how she began identifying as a feminist over time.

We also get more insight into Mariame's philosophy regarding political change; her belief in the capacity for growth and evolution draws from many sources. In a 2019 interview with Chicago-based poet, writer, and scholar Eve L. Ewing, we are treated to a rare public exploration of Mariame's family history, including her father's involvement in Guinea's independence movement and post-independence politics, and her mother's mutual aid work. Mariame reflects on how her parents and upbringing inform her political philosophy, especially regarding the overlapping practices of relationship building, collective care, and abolition. As shared with Ewing, Mariame's father impressed upon her, "Everything that is worthwhile is done with other people." As Mariame notes, that "became the soundtrack in my head," and is articulated in both her organizing work as well as her reflections on the current political moment as more people seek to understand abolition and hopefully get involved.

Her pithy tweets widely circulate and are often quoted, but as we see in *We Do This 'Til We Free Us*, they are informed by consistent study, reflection, and an interest in being moved as much as moving others. For example, Mariame is known for the aphorism "Hope is a discipline." As Mariame reveals in an interview for the podcast *Beyond Prisons*, the four-word phrase articulates a philosophy she was introduced to by a nun that has since become "really helpful in my practice around organizing. I believe that there's always a potential for transformation and for change."

As Mariame shows time and time again, "a potential for transformation and for change" cannot just be the basis of positive rhetoric, but must be enacted—this involves risk. And in short, we must experiment. To this end, several pieces in this book seek to inform readers of how we can practice abolitionist organizing. Whether the battle and historic victory for reparations for survivors of police torture in Chicago, the campaign to hold Chicago Police Department officer Dante Servin accountable for the murder of Rekia Boyd, defense campaigns for criminalized and incarcerated survivors like Marissa Alexander, the #NoCopAcademy campaign in Chicago, and, in response to the murder of Breonna Taylor, a call for reparations and repair rather than the prosecution of officers—all are committed to abolitionist praxis.

In some of the interviews conducted during the summer of 2020, Mariame is asked about the co-optation of the abolitionist movement or performativity versus real politics. What we see in Mariame's responses is her desire to bring as many people to the movement as possible. As Toni Cade Bambara wrote of emerging writers, Mariame expresses of people participating in abolitionist work: they "have to be given space to breathe and stumble. They have to be given time to develop and to reveal what they can do. . . . There are no soloists after all; this is group improvisation."

For Mariame, group improvisation means working together, learning together, and failing together by "building a million different little experiments, just building and trying and taking risks and understanding we're going to have tons of failure." While Mariame encourages experimentation and being open to failure, she remains steadfast that abolitionist politics requires certain principles, such as seeking accountability for harm and violence without involving or expanding the prison-industrial complex. Mariame also notes that practicing abolition demands healthy ego checks in terms of not confusing our feelings for policy or politics.

Mariame Kaba, the writer

In her interview, Ewing asks Mariame about her increased visibility, as she is well known for not wanting her face to appear in photos or videos: "I saw a picture of you in *The New York Times,* and I was like, 'Oh, my goodness.' . . . I would love to hear your thoughts around why you generally choose to not be photographed, and some of your other choices around naming yourself, not centering yourself. And then ways in which that is changing, and why." Mariame's response reveals that she is pushing herself to take credit for her work. She tells a story, the details of which I won't spoil here, that "began the shift in my life around putting my name on my stuff."

When I read Mariame's reply to Ewing, I remembered the first time I learned of Mariame's resistance to putting her name on things. Years ago, when we still hadn't met in person, I wanted to tag her and post something on Twitter from *Prison Culture: How the PIC Structures Our World,* the blog she has published since 2010 that explores "the many arms of the carceral state and how we might dismantle our current systems of punishment." Because she did not have her name as part of her Twitter bio (and still doesn't!), I messaged to ask if I should include her name. She was fine with the post being shared but preferred to not have her name included. As someone who prefers lower frequencies, I was intrigued but didn't ask. Years later, when I first met Mariame in person, I would gain more insight into her citation practices. As we dined on

Indian food, she told parts of the story she shares with Ewing.

As Ewing prefaces her interview, "It is no surprise that many of those struggling to believe in something in the face of despair have turned to the work of educator and organizer Mariame Kaba. Many (myself included) came to her first through *Prison Culture*." Like Ewing, I first became familiar with Mariame as a writer through her blog.

That Mariame blogged regularly is significant for a few reasons. First, she is busy organizing and educating, sometimes teaching college classes, and constantly creating curricula, developing and facilitating workshops and trainings, and providing mentorship, particularly to younger organizers. Second, as Mariame frequently shares publicly, she does not like writing and makes herself do it. This might seem a pedestrian point as other writers, including those recognized as literary giants, express the same sentiment. Yet rarely in public profiles will you see Mariame describe herself as a writer. She is more likely to let you know she is a Hallmark Channel devotee.

Some of her writing circulates widely through social media and email, such as her articles, essays, tweets, and Facebook posts. Some are books, like *Missing Daddy*, written for children with fathers in prison and illustrated by bria royal, and her coauthored book with Essence McDowell, *Lifting as They Climbed: Mapping a History of Black Women on Chicago's South Side*. Other writings include her blog, zines, organizing guides and toolkits, curriculum, research reports, and emails in which she responds to requests for guidance from those getting involved in political work for the first time or seasoned organizers reaching out to a comrade. With some of her writing, Mariame's name does not appear. Nevertheless, she wrote it.

And there is a whole other body of Mariame's writing—not included in this book—that appears in academic publications, produced while she was a sociology graduate student at Northwestern University. Her move to Chicago to attend graduate school brought Mariame to the city that would be her political home and the site of many of her abolitionist experiments for decades. Unsurprisingly, Chicago—and the relationships, organizations, and campaigns Mariame built in the city—are featured in much of her writing. It is here we see Mariame making connections between the international, the national, and the local while always being present in a particular way in the city in which she lives. After all, as Mariame notes, abolitionist practice involves getting to know your neighbors.

So why has Mariame written so much if she detests writing? And when it's often—but not always—done solo? In addition to writing that advances organizations (such as Project Nia or Interrupting Criminalization) and writing to support campaigns, Mariame is practicing what she preaches to fellow organizers: document your work and write yourself into the record. Mariame encourages organizers to do so, despite any attention given to them by journalists, pundits, and academics, as many from the outside might not get it right. In doing so, Mariame has joined a publishing history of Black women organizers and activists who wrote themselves into the archives, including Mary Church Terrell and Ida B. Wells-Barnett.

As Mariame shares in her interview with Ewing, Wells-Barnett is a major touchstone. Like Wells-Barnett, Mariame spent many formative years in Chicago. Shamefully, Wells-Barnett was initially written out of the political historiography of anti-lynching organizing by contemporaries who knew better. But Mariame's political work and writings have, at least recently, received considerable attention—partly aided by her adroit, lively presence on social media. And unlike those who sought to write autobiographies reviewing their lives, Mariame is writing herself into the record as a simultaneous exploration of organizing, archiving, and thinking through ideas and next steps.

Read this urgent and revelatory book, and see for yourself—Mariame Kaba is a serious organizer, thinker, and writer. She engages and produces ideas in the course of political organizing, building relationships, and waging campaigns. She thinks through her work. A lot. She studies. She reflects. She struggles. She experiments. She rethinks. She writes. She and her work are always "moving toward the horizon of abolition." Read this book, and move toward the horizon with her.

PART I

So You're Thinking about Becoming an Abolitionist

So You're Thinking about Becoming an Abolitionist

LEVEL, October 2020

Today, more people are discussing and contemplating prison abolition than ever before. Decades of collective organizing have brought us to this moment: some are newly aware that prisons, policing, and the criminal punishment system in general are racist, oppressive, and ineffective.

However, some might be wondering, "Is abolition too drastic? Can we really get rid of prisons and policing all together?" The short answer: We can. We must. We are.

Prison-industrial complex abolition is a political vision, a structural analysis of oppression, and a practical organizing strategy. While some people might think of abolition as primarily a negative project—"Let's tear everything down tomorrow and hope for the best"—PIC abolition is a vision of a restructured society in a world where we have everything we need: food, shelter, education, health, art, beauty, clean water, and more things that are foundational to our personal and community safety.

Every vision is also a map. As freedom fighter Kwame Ture taught us, "When you see people call themselves revolutionary always talking about destroying, destroying, destroying but never talking about building or creating, they're not revolutionary. They do not understand the first thing about revolution. It's creating." PIC abolition is a positive project that focuses, in part, on building a society where it is possible to address harm without relying on structural forms of oppression or the violent systems that increase it.

Some people may ask, "Does this mean that I can never call the cops if my life is in serious danger?" Abolition does not center that

2

question. Instead, abolition challenges us to ask "Why do we have no other well-resourced options?" and pushes us to creatively consider how we can grow, build, and try other avenues to reduce harm. Repeated attempts to improve the sole option offered by the state, despite how consistently corrupt and injurious it has proven itself, will neither reduce nor address the harm that actually required the call. We need more and effective options for the greatest number of people.

Let's begin our abolitionist journey not with the question "What do we have now, and how can we make it better?" Instead, let's ask, "What can we imagine for ourselves and the world?" If we do that, then boundless possibilities of a more just world await us.

An abolitionist journey ignites other questions capable of meaningful and transformative pathways: What work do prisons and policing actually do? Most people assume that incarceration helps to reduce violence and crime, thinking, "The criminal punishment system might be racist, sexist, classist, ableist, and unfair, but it at least keeps me safe from violence and crime."

Facts and history tell a different story: Increasing rates of incarceration have a minimal impact on crime rates. Research and common sense suggest that economic precarity is correlated with higher crime rates. Moreover, crime and harm are not synonymous. All that is criminalized isn't harmful, and all harm isn't necessarily criminalized. For example, wage theft by employers isn't generally criminalized, but it is definitely harmful.

Even if the criminal punishment system were free of racism, classism, sexism, and other isms, it would not be capable of effectively addressing harm. For example, if we want to reduce (or end) sexual and gendered violence, putting a few perpetrators in prison does little to stop the many other perpetrators. It does nothing to change a culture that makes this harm imaginable, to hold the individual perpetrator accountable, to support their transformation, or to meet the needs of the survivors.

A transformative justice movement led by Black, Indigenous, and people of color survivors has emerged in the past two decades to offer a different vision for ending violence and transforming our communities.

A world without harm isn't possible and isn't what an abolitionist vision purports to achieve. Rather, abolitionist politics and practice contend that disposing of people by locking them away in jails and prisons does nothing significant to prevent, reduce, or transform harm in the aggregate. It rarely, if ever, encourages people to take accountability for their actions. Instead, our adversarial court system discourages people from ever acknowledging, let alone taking responsibility for, the harm they have caused. At the same time, it allows us to avoid our own responsibilities to hold each other accountable, instead delegating it to a third party—one that has been built to hide away social and political failures. An abolitionist imagination takes us along a different path than if we try to simply replace the PIC with similar structures.

None of us has all of the answers, or we would have ended oppression already. But if we keep building the world we want, trying new things, and learning from our mistakes, new possibilities emerge.

Here's how to begin.

First, when we set about trying to transform society, we must remember that we ourselves will also need to transform. Our imagination of what a different world can be is limited. We are deeply entangled in the very systems we are organizing to change. White supremacy, misogyny, ableism, classism, homophobia, and transphobia exist everywhere. We have all so thoroughly internalized these logics of oppression that if oppression were to end tomorrow, we would be likely to reproduce previous structures. Being intentionally in relation to one another, a part of a collective, helps to not only imagine new worlds, but also to imagine ourselves differently. Join some of the many organizations, faith groups, and ad hoc collectives that are working to learn and unlearn, for example, what it feels like to actually be safe or those that are naming and challenging white supremacy and racial capitalism.

Second, we must imagine and experiment with new collective structures that enable us to take more principled action, such as embracing collective responsibility to resolve conflicts. We can learn lessons from revolutionary movements, like Brazil's Landless Workers Movement (Movimento dos Trabalhadores Rurais Sem Terra), that have noted that when we create social structures that are less hierarchical and more transparent, we reduce violence and harms.

Third, we must simultaneously engage in strategies that reduce contact between people and the criminal legal system. Abolitionists regularly engage in organizing campaigns and mutual aid efforts that move us closer to our goals. We must remember that the goal is not to create a gentler prison and policing system because, as I have noted, a gentler prison and policing system cannot adequately address harm. Instead, we want to divest from these systems as we create the world in which we want to live.

Fourth, as scholar and activist Ruth Wilson Gilmore notes, building a different world requires that we not only change how we address harm but also that we change everything. The PIC is linked in its logics and operation with all other systems—from how students are pushed out of schools when they don't perform as expected to how people with disabilities are excluded from our communities and the ways in which workers are treated as expendable in our capitalist system.

Changing everything might sound daunting, but it also means there are many places to start, infinite opportunities to collaborate, and endless imaginative interventions and experiments to create. Let's begin our abolitionist journey not with the question "What do we have now, and how can we make it better?" Instead, let's ask, "What can we imagine for ourselves and the world?" If we do that, then boundless possibilities of a more just world await us.

The System Isn't Broken

The New Inquiry, June 2015

"Ms. K, they got me again."

Six words set up the familiar routine. A car ride to the station. An unwanted and unwelcome conversation with the officer at the desk. Rudeness, contempt, and that awful perma-smirk. Waiting in anticipation; false alarms. A reprieve: an escape without ransom. More waiting. Finally, the bowed head and slumped shoulders of a young Black man walking toward me. No tears. Where are the tears? Another court date or maybe not. Another record to expunge, always. Then it starts all over again.

I dread summer. It's the season of hypersurveillance and even more aggressive policing of young people of color in my neighborhood.

The urban summer criminalization merry-go-round—a kind of demented child's play. Quotidian terrorism in the service of law and order. Low-intensity police riots against young Black people. My anecdotal observations are supported by empirical data. The ACLU of Illinois says that last summer, based on population, Chicago police made "far more street stops than New York City police did at the height of their use of stop-and-frisk. The CPD stopped more than 250,000 innocent people." Unsurprisingly, the vast majority of those stops involved Black people who, while making up 32 percent of Chicago's population, were 72 percent of the stops.

Some studies suggest a correlation between summer and a rise in "crime." I can hear the justifications: "If crime increases in the summer, then more police aggression is justified." This fails to take into account that "routine" interactions between police and young people in my community are fraught all year long. Summer exacerbates these oppressive contacts, because many more young people are out of school and usually without jobs, hanging out in public spaces.

Public spaces in urban and suburban towns are contested. Residents collude with law enforcement to police and enforce boundaries. Young people of color are criminalized not only by the police but also by community members.

Yesterday yet another video went viral on social media. It depicts police officers in McKinney, Texas, swarming a pool party filled with teenagers, and one particular officer manhandling a fourteen-year-old Black girl wearing a bikini. The young people are cursed at, have a gun pointed at them, and are taunted for being afraid of the cops. Fifteen-year-old Miles Jai Thomas explains what happened:

> "So, a cop grabbed her arm and flipped her to the ground after she and him were arguing about him cursing at us," Thomas said.
>
> When two teens went toward the cop to help the girl, they were accused of sneaking up on the cop to attack.
>
> "So, a cop yelled 'get those motherfuckers' and they chased [us] with guns out. That's why in the video I started running," Thomas said.
>
> "I was scared because all I could think was, 'Don't shoot me,'" he said.

Watching the video, I was struck by how the young people were denied the right to be afraid. Their fear was illegitimate. And it makes sense; only human beings are allowed to be afraid. For the cops, these youth of color (mostly Black) are not human.

I dread summer.

I attended a conference recently about youth–police interactions. The familiar trope about the need for young people and the cops to get to know each other was bandied about, useless pablum offered as a solution for ending police violence, which relies on a faulty definition of the problem. As a young person once told me: "I know the cops here very well, and they know me. We know each other too well. That's not the problem. The problem is that they harass me daily. If they'd stop that, we'd be fine." The young people in my community who come into contact with the police can recite their names and badge numbers. Those are unforgettable to them; the stuff of their nightmares. It's unclear to me how more conversations will change the dynamics of such oppression. For most of the public, whether liberal or conservative, it's the cops' job to arrest people, and they are incentivized to do that work. Presumably, then, what would need to change to shift the dynamics are the job descriptions and the incentives.

A persistent and seemingly endemic feature of US society is the conflation of Blackness and criminality. William Patterson, a well-known Black communist, wrote in 1970, "A false brand of criminality is constantly stamped on the brow of Black youth by the courts and systematically kept there creating the fiction that blacks are a criminally minded people." He added that "the lies against blacks are propped up ideologically." I would suggest that they are also maintained and enforced through force and violence.

When Baltimore police dressed in riot gear turned their violence on high school students at the Mondawmin Mall a few weeks ago, some people were horrified. "These are children," onlookers exclaimed on social media. I thought grimly of how the cops would see the situation. There are no children here; only targets and threats. Social science research suggests that cops see Black children as older and as less innocent than their white peers. The research confirms what most of us already know—Black children are considered to be disposable and dangerous mini-adults.

This is not new. I came across the story of thirteen-year-old Beverly Lee when I read the 1951 "We Charge Genocide" petition many years ago. Lee was shot in the back by a Detroit police officer on October 12, 1947. Here's the item that piqued my interest as it appeared in "We Charge Genocide":

> Beverly Lee, 13-year-old youth, was shot to death by Policeman Louis Begin of Detroit, Michigan. Mrs. Francis Vonbatten of 1839 Pine testified that she saw Lee and another walking down the street, and saw the squad car approach. She heard, "Stop, you little so-and-so," and then a shot. The officer was subsequently cleared by Coroner Lloyd K. Babcock.

I was particularly interested in the incident because I thought that Beverly was a girl, and police violence cases involving Black girls and young women have been overlooked. In fact, I haven't found any historical incidents of police violence against Black women and girls that led to mass mobilization. Current campaigns, such as #SayHerName, point to the enduring erasure of state violence against Black girls and women.

The incident in McKinney, Texas, featured physical violence against a Black girl, underscoring the fact that girls (cis and trans) are consistently at risk of law enforcement abuse. On further research, I learned that Beverly Lee was actually a boy. On the day after Beverly Lee was shot, the *Detroit News* reported on the incident:

> Shot in the back as he tried to evade arrest, a seventh-grade schoolboy was killed by a Detroit patrolman late Sunday. The boy, Beverly Lee, 13, of 2637 Twelfth Street, was shot by Patrolman Louis Begin, of the Trumbull station, when he disregarded orders to halt. Begin and his partner, Patrolman William Owens, were called to Temple and Vermont avenues where Mrs. Mabel Gee, 1930 Temple, reported her purse stolen. Approaching the intersection, they saw Lee, ordered him to halt, and Owens fired a warning shot. Begin shot him as he continued to run away from the scout car. A watch belonging to Mrs. Gee and $18, the amount she said was in her purse, were found in the boy's pockets. The purse was recovered nearby. Begin and Owens made statements to William D. Brusstar, assistant prosecutor. They said Mrs. Gee referred to her assailant as a *man* and, when they encountered him, they thought he was an adult [emphasis mine]. Lee was about five feet, six inches tall. Other victims of recent purse snatchings were being invited to view the body at the County Morgue. Lee attended Condon Intermediate School. His body was identified by his mother, Mrs. Leah Lee.

The discrepancy between these two accounts is unsurprising. As we have so often seen, there is usually a variance between initial press reports and official police accounts and community narratives. Notice that the cops and the alleged robbery victim said that they thought Lee was an adult. The adultification of Black children has long and deep roots that date back to chattel slavery. In fact, before the Civil War, half of all enslaved people were under sixteen years old. Enslaved children were property and were expected to work; children as young as six years old worked the fields.

Beverly Lee was the third Black boy killed by police that year in Detroit. Community members were furious and organized protests over Lee's killing. Despite the uproar, only eight days after the shooting, the prosecutor closed the investigation into Lee's death, calling it "justifiable homicide." The Detroit NAACP met with the prosecutor and called for an inquest into the facts to the case. They presented him with signed statements of witnesses contradicting his findings. It appears that the community, led by the NAACP, continued to organize around Lee's case without success; charges were not brought against Officer Begin. Police impunity has a long history in this country. In the end, a thirteen-year-old Black boy was shot in the back by police and died. To quote Ossie Davis, Black people understand that "we live with death and it is ours."

Most often, it's police shootings and killings that spark urban uprisings. However, the daily indignities and more invisible harms are ever-present and are the foundation of hostilities between young people of color and police. Routine state violence carried out by the police happens outside of public view, under the guise of addressing gun and other forms of violence. If past is prologue, my community can look forward to another summer of intense, relentless, and surely illegal police harassment of young people of color, and specifically of young Black men.

Young people riding their bikes on sidewalks, instead of being ticketed as prescribed by law, will be hauled into police lockups. They'll be accused of resisting arrest and then funneled into Cook County Jail. Teenagers leaving summer programming will be followed by cop cars, and asked where they are heading. One cross word will lead to being roughly thrown on car hoods in front of the whole neighborhood. Walking through alleys as shortcuts to head home from work, young people will be hounded, provoked, and dragged to the station. But not before being beaten in the car, without any concern for health conditions like seizures. Trans and gender nonconforming youth will be bullied and verbally harassed for walking down the street. Young people will be picked up without cause and driven into rival gang territory to be dumped without wallets or phones—only to hear the cops announce for all to hear that they belong to the rival gang. Young women walking down the street minding their own business will be sexually harassed by those sworn to "protect and serve."

I dread summer.

Besides stop-and-frisks and other violations, young people in my community are also subjected to warrantless searches of their homes.

One young person I know narrated his experience in the 2014 *We Charge Genocide* report to the United Nations Committee against Torture:

> We're sitting in a house playing video games, and we hear a bang-ing on the door. Before we know it, the door is kicked down and there's five special-ops officers with their huge M16s drawn, pointed at us—three 15-year-olds playing video games. And they tell us get on the ground. They say if we move, they are gonna kill us; "Don't look at me, we'll fucking kill you in a second!" Pointing their guns at us. Then they don't find anything. They let us all go, they laugh, try to joke with us, apologize, then leave out. And we're sitting there like, "What just happened?" They tear up the house. They stole money.

Lest you think that this is an innovation of zero-tolerance militarized policing born out of the war on drugs, here's an example from eighty years ago. When the people of Harlem rioted in 1935, it was once again an incident of police violence that lit the fuse. A rumor that Lino Rivera, a sixteen-year-old Black Puerto Rican young man, was killed by New York City Police led to nearly four thousand Harlemites taking to the streets. Seven hundred police officers were dispatched to the community. When all was said and done, three people had died, and more than $200 million in damages were sustained from the riot. In the aftermath, Mayor LaGuardia commissioned a report to understand the causes of the up-rising. In a section titled "The Police in Harlem," the report's authors maintained that cops routinely entered the homes of Black Harlemites "without a warrant and searched them at will." Instead of drugs, Harlem cops in the 1930s were searching for policy slips in efforts to crack down on illegal gambling. Reprinted in the report was a letter by a Harlem res-ident addressed to the mayor. Below are a few excerpts:

> On Tuesday morning, April 16, 1935, between 10 and 11 o'clock, the superintendent of the house rapped at my door. Upon opening it, I was confronted with three men (men in civilian clothes) who the superintendent said were policemen. He explained that the men were searching the house, for what he did not know.
>
> The men entered the room, and proceeded to search without showing shields or search warrant. I asked twice of two of the men what was the reason for such action. I received no answer from any of them.

My dresser drawers were thoroughly gone into, dresser cover even being raised. My bed came in for similar search, covers were dragged off and mattress overturned. Suitcase under my bed was brought up and searched. My overcoat hanging on the door was gone over and into. My china closet was opened and glassware examined. After this startling act the men left my room, still without saying a word.

These types of violations span centuries for Black people and are one reason for racial disconnects in discussions about privacy and civil liberties. Black people have always been under the gaze of the state, and we know that our rights are routinely violable. Civil liberties and individual rights have different meanings for different groups of people. They also have different priorities, depending on social contexts. A review of Black history suggests that considerations of civil liberties are always embedded within concepts of equality and social justice. In other words, by design or necessity, Black people have focused on our collective rights over our individual liberties. This makes sense in a society where we don't just assume individual Black guilt and suspicion; we are all guilty and we are all suspicious (even if we may want to deny this reality). In that context, individual liberties and rights take a back seat to a collective struggle for emancipation and freedom. Additionally, as a people, we have always known that it is impossible for us to exercise our individual rights within a context of more generalized social, economic, and political oppression.

History offers evidence of the intractability of the problem of police violence. What should we do then? Quite simply, we must end the police. The hegemony of police is so complete that we often can't begin to imagine a world without the institution. We are too reliant on the police. In fact, the police increase their legitimacy through all of the non-police-related work that they assume, including doing wellness and mental health checks. Why should armed people be deployed to do the work of community members and social workers? Why have we become so comfortable with ceding so much power to the police? Any discussion of reform must begin with the following questions: how will we decrease the numbers of police, and how will we defund the institution?

On the way to abolition, we can take a number of intermediate steps to shrink the police force and to restructure our relationships with each other. These include:

1) Organizing for dramatic decreases of police budgets and redirecting those funds to other social goods (defunding the police).

2) Ending cash bail.

3) Overturning police bills of rights.

4) Abolishing police unions.

5) Crowding out the police in our communities.

6) Disarming the police.

7) Creating abolitionist messages that penetrate the public consciousness to disrupt the idea that cops = safety.

8) Building community-based interventions that address harms without relying on police.

9) Evaluating any reforms based on these criteria.

10) Thinking through the end of the police and imagining alternatives.

Importantly, we must reject all talk about policing and the overall criminal punishment system being "broken" or "not working." By rhetorically constructing the criminal punishment system as "broken," reform is reaffirmed and abolition is painted as unrealistic and unworkable. Those of us who maintain that reform is actually impossible within the current context are positioned as unreasonable and naive. Ideological formations often operate invisibly to delineate and define what is acceptable discourse. Challenges to dominant ideological formations about "justice" are met with anger, ridicule, or are simply ignored. This is in the service of those who benefit from the current system and works to enforce white supremacy and anti-Blackness. The losers under this injustice system are the young people I know and love.

I really dread summer . . .

Yes, We Mean Literally Abolish the Police

The New York Times, June 2020

Congressional Democrats want to make it easier to identify and prosecute police misconduct; Joe Biden wants to give police departments $300 million. But efforts to solve police violence through liberal reforms like these have failed for nearly a century.

Enough. We can't reform the police. The only way to diminish police violence is to reduce contact between the public and the police.

There is not a single era in United States history in which the police were not a force of violence against Black people. Policing in the South emerged from the slave patrols in the 1700s and 1800s that caught and returned runaway slaves. In the North, the first municipal police departments in the mid-1800s helped quash labor strikes and riots against the rich. Everywhere, police have suppressed marginalized populations to protect the status quo.

So, when you see a police officer pressing his knee into a Black man's neck until he dies, that's the logical result of policing in America. When a police officer brutalizes a Black person, he is doing what he sees as his job. Now two weeks of nationwide protests have led some to call for defunding the police, while others argue that doing so would make us less safe.

The first thing to point out is that police officers don't do what you think they do. They spend most of their time responding to noise complaints, issuing parking and traffic citations, and dealing with other noncriminal issues. We've been taught to think they "catch the bad guys; they chase the bank robbers; they find the serial killers," said Alex Vitale, the coordinator of the Policing and Social Justice Project at Brooklyn College, in an interview with *Jacobin*. But this is "a big myth," he said. "The vast majority of police officers make one felony arrest a year. If they make two, they're cop of the month."

We can't simply change their job descriptions to focus on the worst of the worst criminals. That's not what they are set up to do. Second, a safe world is not one in which the police keep Black and other marginalized people in check through threats of arrest, incarceration, violence, and death.

I've been advocating the abolition of the police for years. Regardless of your view on police power—whether you want to get rid of the police or simply to make them less violent—here's an immediate demand we can all make: cut the number of police in half and cut their budget in half. Fewer police officers equals fewer opportunities for them to brutalize and kill people. The idea is gaining traction in Minneapolis, Dallas, Los Angeles, and other cities.

History is instructive, not because it offers us a blueprint for how to act in the present, but because it can help us ask better questions for the future.

The Lexow Committee undertook the first major investigation into police misconduct in New York City in 1894. At the time, the most common complaint against the police was about "clubbing"—"the routine bludgeoning of citizens by patrolmen armed with nightsticks or Blackjacks," as the historian Marilynn Johnson has written.

The Wickersham Commission, convened to study the criminal justice system and examine the problem of Prohibition enforcement, offered a scathing indictment in 1931, including evidence of brutal interrogation strategies. It put the blame on a lack of professionalism among the police.

After the 1967 urban uprisings, the Kerner Commission found that "police actions were 'final' incidents before the outbreak of violence in 12 of the 24 surveyed disorders." Its report listed a now-familiar set of recommendations, like working to build "community support for law enforcement" and reviewing police operations "in the ghetto, to ensure proper conduct by police officers."

These commissions didn't stop the violence; they just served as a kind of counterinsurgent function each time police violence led to protests. Calls for similar reforms were trotted out in response to the brutal police beating of Rodney King in 1991 and the rebellion that followed, and again after the killings of Michael Brown and Eric Garner.

The Obama administration's *Final Report of the President's Task Force on 21st Century Policing* resulted in procedural tweaks like implicit-bias training, police-community listening sessions, slight alterations of use-of-force policies, and systems to identify potentially problematic officers early on.

But even a member of the task force, Tracey Meares, noted in 2017, "Policing as we know it must be abolished before it can be transformed."

The philosophy undergirding these reforms is that more rules will mean less violence. But police officers break rules all the time. Look what has happened over the past few weeks—police officers slashing tires, shoving old men on camera, and arresting and injuring journalists and protesters. These officers are not worried about repercussions any more than Daniel Pantaleo, the former New York City police officer whose chokehold led to Eric Garner's death; he waved to a camera filming the incident. He knew that the police union would back him up, and he was right. He stayed on the job for five more years.

Minneapolis had instituted many of these "best practices" but failed to remove Derek Chauvin from the force despite seventeen misconduct complaints over nearly two decades, culminating in the entire world watching as he knelt on George Floyd's neck for almost nine minutes. Why on earth would we think the same reforms would work now? We need to change our demands. The surest way of reducing police violence is to reduce the power of the police, by cutting budgets and the number of officers.

But don't get me wrong. We are not abandoning our communities to violence. We don't want to just close police departments. We want to make them obsolete.

We should redirect the billions that now go to police departments toward providing health care, housing, education, and good jobs. If we did this, there would be less need for the police in the first place.

We can build other ways of responding to harms in our society. Trained community care workers could do mental-health checks if someone needs help. Towns could use restorative justice models instead of throwing people in prison.

What about rape? The current approach hasn't ended it. In fact, most rapists never see the inside of a courtroom. Two-thirds of people who experience sexual violence never report it to anyone. Those who file police reports are often dissatisfied with the response. Additionally, police officers themselves commit sexual assault alarmingly often. A study in 2010 found that sexual misconduct was the second most frequently reported form of police misconduct. In 2015, the *Buffalo News* found that an officer was caught for sexual misconduct every five days.

When people, especially white people, consider a world without the police, they envision a society as violent as our current one, merely without law enforcement—and they shudder. As a society, we have been so indoctrinated with the idea that we solve problems by policing and caging people that many cannot imagine anything other than prisons and the police as solutions to violence and harm.

People like me who want to abolish prisons and police, however, have a vision of a different society, built on cooperation instead of individualism, on mutual aid instead of self-preservation. What would the country look like if it had billions of extra dollars to spend on housing, food, and education for all? This change in society wouldn't happen immediately, but the protests show that many people are ready to embrace a different vision of safety and justice.

When the streets calm and people suggest once again that we hire more Black police officers or create more civilian review boards, I hope that we remember all the times those efforts have failed.

A Jailbreak of the Imagination:
Seeing Prisons for What They Are
and Demanding Transformation

with Kelly Hayes

Truthout, May 2018

Our current historical moment demands a radical reimagining of how we address various harms. The levers of power are currently in the hands of an administration that is openly hostile to the most marginalized in our society (Black people, Native people, the poor, LGBTQ people, immigrant communities, and more). While we protect ourselves from their consistent and regular blows, we must also fight for a vision of the world we want to inhabit.

For us, that's a world where people like Tiffany Rusher, who began a five-year sentence at Logan Correctional Center in Broadwell Township, Illinois, in 2013, are not tortured to death in the name of "safety." Our vision insists on the abolition of the prison-industrial complex as a critical pillar of the creation of a new society.

Imprisoned on charges related to sex work, Tiffany Rusher was eventually placed in solitary confinement for getting into a physical struggle with one of her cellmates. During her time in solitary confinement, Rusher's mental health began to deteriorate, initiating a cycle of self-harm. After a series of suicide attempts and periods of solitary confinement, Rusher was placed on "crisis watch" for a period of eight months.

According to Rusher's lawyer, Alan Mills, being on crisis watch meant being stripped of all clothing and belongings, and placed in a bare cell with only a "suicide smock" (a single piece of thick woven ny-

18

lon, too stiff to fold, with holes for one's head and arms). During this time, Rusher was monitored through a plexiglass wall, with the lights on, twenty-four hours a day. Rather than receiving mental health care, Rusher was kept naked, except for her rigid smock, in an empty cell. She was given strict, dehumanizing instructions about how to wipe herself and manage her menstrual hygiene, which included a requirement that her hands be visible to the guard watching her at all times. In order to read, Rusher had to persuade a prison guard to hold an open book against the glass of her cell, and turn each page as she finished reading it.

As time wore on, Rusher asked her attorney: "Who in her situation wouldn't want to kill themselves?"

At the end of her sentence, Rusher was finally transferred to a mental health facility. Rusher, who disclosed to her doctors that she had experienced childhood sexual abuse, had received dozens of diagnoses over the years, including schizoaffective disorder, but nonetheless made great strides while in treatment. Eight months into her in-patient care, however, Rusher got into altercation with another patient. Rather than treating the episode as a symptom of her mental health problems, she was sent back to jail, where the cycle of carceral violence continued.

After Rusher's death, her mother, Kelli Andrews, said in a statement, "Tiffany was a beautiful soul with hopes for her future. She was looking forward to coming home to be with her family. We miss her every day." Sangamon County jail returned Rusher to solitary confinement, where she remained for three months before being found unresponsive with a ripped piece of a towel around her neck. Rusher died twelve days later when the hospital removed her from life support. In the words of Mills, "First they tortured her, then they killed her."

At the time of her death, Tiffany Rusher was twenty-seven years old.

Sadly, what Rusher endured was not exceptional. The US prison system is designed to crush people like Tiffany Rusher every day, with only a small section of society laboring to help prisoners save themselves from being ground under. In Rusher's case, the attorneys and staff of Uptown People's Law Center in Chicago were her defenders, but, in the end, the wounds inflicted by the system were too deep, and the cycle of carceral violence was simply too entrenched to interrupt. Rusher, now a statistic to the world at large and a court filing to those her attorneys would hold accountable for her death, was refused any recognition of her humanity while incarcerated. But Rusher was not a number. She was a human being, and restoring our awareness of the humanity of prisoners is a crucial step toward undoing the harms of mass incarceration.

As prison abolitionists, grassroots organizers, and practitioners of transformative justice, our vision for 2018 is one of clear-eyed awareness and discussion of the horrors of the prison system—and the action that awareness demands. As a society, we have long turned away from any social concern that overwhelms us. Whether it's war, climate change, or the prison-industrial complex, Americans have been conditioned to simply look away from profound harms. Years of this practice have now left us with endless wars, dying oceans, and millions of people in bondage and oppressively policed. It is time for a thorough, unflinching examination of what our society has wrought and what we have become. It is time to envision and create alternatives to the hellish conditions our society has brought into being.

The Illusion of a New Idea

Outspoken opponents of abolishing the prison-industrial complex typically portray abolitionists as politically inactive academics who spout impossible ideas. None of this could be further from the truth. Abolitionists come from all backgrounds, and most are politically active. From bail reform to strategic electoral interventions and mutual aid, prison abolitionists are steadily at work in our communities, employing tactics of harm reduction, lobbying for and against legislation, defending the rights of prisoners in solidarity with those organizing for themselves on the inside, and working to forward a vision of social transformation.

As a political framework, abolition has gained significant ground in recent years, with groups like the National Lawyers Guild adopting the philosophy in their work. A growing number of grassroots abolitionist organizers have co-organized nationally recognized campaigns such as the #ByeAnita effort in Chicago, which helped to successfully remove former state's attorney Anita Alvarez from office. Abolitionist organizers also helped lead efforts to win reparations for survivors of torture that occurred under the now infamous police commander Jon

Burge in Chicago—a city that has, over the past two decades, become a hub of abolitionist organizing. Abolition is a practical organizing strategy.

Like any enterprise that was born of a manufactured demand, prisons perpetuate themselves, and that requires the maintenance of conditions that foster crime. From 1978 to 2014, the US prison population rose 408 percent, largely filling its cages with those denied access to education, employment, and human services. About 70 percent of prisoners in California are former foster care youth. And given that the system is actually geared toward recidivism, there can be no argument that the prison system supports either public safety or the public good. Our failure to build a culture of care that nurtures human growth and potential, rather than incubating desperation, ensures that more "criminals" will be created and subsequently punished, to the great benefit of those who profit from industries associated with incarceration. Prison is simply a bad and ineffective way to address violence and crime.

Yet when we speak about the abolition of the prison-industrial complex, many react as though the idea is alien and unthinkable—as if, to them, prisons, policing and surveillance are part of a natural order that simply cannot be undone. In truth, the prison system did not see its most massive population surge until the 1980s, when deindustrialization created the need for dungeon economies to replace lost jobs, and a backlash against the Civil Rights Movement and other social gains by Black people propelled heightened efforts at social control.

As a society, we have been taught to embrace social control, which is often enforced by people with guns, because we have been taught to fear each other, and to acquiesce to authority. We live in a culture that celebrates criminalization, cops, and prisons. Abusive, torturous police become sympathetic television characters whose harms the public can understand or even sympathize with. But when a civilian has committed an egregious harm, the national solace we are taught to seek is to see them suffer. They must be thrown in a cage, and, once they are, justice is considered to be done, and we can all move on with our lives without ever asking questions like: Why did this happen? Why does it keep happening? And is there something we could change that would make this tragedy unthinkable in the first place?

Clapping for Incarceration

Even those who acknowledge that mass incarceration in the US is nightmarish and unjust often feel compelled to applaud when the system ensnares someone whose harms disgust us. When Martin Shkreli, a former hedge fund manager, was sentenced to serve seven years for securities fraud, memes and laughter abounded. Shkreli, who famously engaged in pharmaceutical price-gauging, raising the price of the drug Daraprim from $13.50 to $750 per pill, was once characterized as the "most hated man in America," making him an ideal poster child for the carceral state. But like most ideas that allow us to avert our eyes and ignore the larger system, this notion is full of holes.

For one, Shkreli was not being punished for forcing AIDS patients to pay hundreds of thousands of dollars a year for a lifesaving medication, because rich people simply are not punished for practicing capitalism in the United States. As long as their money changing kills according to the rules of the free market, they see no penalty. Shkreli was punished for securities fraud. In short, he played Monopoly with the filthy rich and broke the rules. Yet, because he also harmed everyday people, this moment is held up as one where the system worked, because someone we feel contempt for was punished. The system will occasionally offer such kernels, but they don't add up to justice.

No reform is being forced upon the pharmaceutical industry in the wake of Shkreli's harms, and the executives who are driving up prices on insulin and other lifesaving medications are not faced with jail time (if this is our marker of justice). Our society's practice of "justice" is not concerned with creating just conditions, and our system of punishment does not penalize the powerful for crushing those with less power. The rich getting richer while others are ground under is part of the "just" order of our society. There are no solutions offered by the system, only the occasional display of suffering or civil death to satisfy the masses.

Given these conditions, we must understand that, by applauding carceral violence, we are also applauding an established and grotesque failure on the part of Western civilization.

Stories like Tiffany Rusher's are buried under headlines about people like Shkreli and serial rapist Larry Nassar—stories that reassure the public that retribution is necessary and that sate a popular desire for vengeance in the face of tragedy and harm. American crime stories are not stories of good versus evil, because the system is not and has never been good or heroic, and criminal harms are usually much more complex than we would care to acknowledge. The crimes for which Tiffany Rusher was convicted involved sex with a minor, but why was Rusher in sexual proximity to a minor in the first place?

Prison is simply a bad and ineffective way to address violence and crime. Cases like Rusher's call on us both to acknowledge the harms our system has inflicted and to create the kind of social and economic conditions in which a young woman would never be presented with the choices that Rusher faced. According to Rusher, she was doing survival sex work when she was solicited to provide sexual services at a party. As it turned out, the young man a relative wanted to purchase sexual favors for was underage. Rusher was twenty-one years old. When the young man's mother learned about the party, she was incensed and filed a police report. And just like that, Rusher became a sex offender in the eyes of the law. However different her experiences may have been from those who are typically characterized as predators, Rusher was ensnared by a damning and unyielding brand of criminalization.

"Dangerous People"

When confronted with statistics about how unevenly criminal penalties are applied in the United States, or with historical evidence that policing and incarceration have always been grounded in anti-Blackness, Native erasure, and protection of property, most leftists will decry the system and agree that change is long overdue. But such admissions are usually followed by an insistence that we cannot simply uproot the system, because we don't have polished, universalized, fully formed solutions to address the dangers some individuals, often characterized as predators, may pose to our communities.

But the idea of "predators" and "dangerous people" is complicated by the conditions our society enforces—social and economic conditions that we know generate crime and despair. Communities whose needs are met are not rife with crimes of desperation, whereas struggling communities are; and people from communities that are highly criminalized by our racist system are far more likely to be thrust into the carceral system.

Politicians routinely feign ignorance with regard to these dynamics, presenting "tough-on-crime" agendas that would enhance prison sentences and widen the school-to-prison pipeline as a solution to the harms society generates. Because if politicians acknowledged that most criminalized harms are rooted in social and economic inequities, they would be expected to address those inequities, which most refuse to do. In the United States, the political careers of elected officials are largely funded by those who directly benefit from the inequities of our society, and those funders would likely abandon their pet officials if they pursued anything resembling economic justice.

The carceral system has always used sensationalized cases and the specter of unthinkable harm to create new mechanisms of disposability. Those mechanisms are what feed bodies to hungry dungeon economies while we are distracted by our own fears of "bad people" and what they might do if they aren't contained. Of course, a system that never addresses the *why* behind a harm never actually contains the harm itself. Cages confine people, not the conditions that facilitated their harms or the mentalities that perpetuate violence. Yet, for some reason, even people who are well versed in the dynamics of the system often believe *Law and Order* moments are possible, when, just for a moment, an instrument of state violence can be made good.

In their essay on "The University and the Undercommons," writers and scholars Fred Moten and Stefano Harney underscore why abolition is important as a political framework and organizing strategy: "What is, so to speak, the object of abolition? Not so much the abolition of prisons but the abolition of a society that could have prisons, that could have slavery, that could have the wage, and therefore not abolition as the elimination of anything but abolition as the founding of a new society." When we look past the sensationalism of major headlines, and examine the actual dynamics of mass incarceration, it becomes increasingly impossible to justify this perspective. While some offer calls for reform, such calls ignore the reality that an institution grounded in the commodification of human beings, through torture and the deprivation of their liberty, cannot be made good. The logic of using policing, punishment, and prison has not proven to address the systemic causes of violence. It is in this climate that we argue that abolition of the prison-industrial complex is the most moral political posture available to us. Because the deconstruction of the American system of mass incarceration is possible, and it is time.

What Does Transformation Look Like?

Our vision for 2018 is a state of unrestrained imagination. When dealing with oppressive systems, cynicism is a begrudging allegiance, extracted from people whose minds could otherwise open new doors, make new demands, and conjure visions of what a better world could look like. Questions like "What about the really dangerous people?" are not questions a prison abolitionist must answer in order to insist the prison-industrial complex must be undone.

These are questions we must collectively answer, even as we trouble the very notion of "dangerousness." The inability to offer a neatly packaged and easily digestible solution does not preclude offering critique or analysis of the ills of our current system.

We live in a society that has been locked into a false sense of inevitability. It's time to look hard at how this system came to be, who profits, how it functions, and why—and it's time to imagine what it would look like to see justice done without relying on punishment and the barbarity of carceral systems. As writer and educator Erica Meiners suggests: "Liberation under oppression is unthinkable by design." It's time for a jailbreak of the imagination in order to make the impossible possible.

Hope Is a Discipline

Interview by Kim Wilson and Brian Sonenstein
Beyond Prisons, January 2018

Kim Wilson: *I think someone retweeted something you posted the other day, and it just really resonated with me and has helped me tremendously. . . . It is something you wrote about hope being a discipline. I got to tell you, it made my day, if not my week, absolutely! Because it is easy to get down on everything that's going on.*

Mariame Kaba: Sure.

Wilson: *It's really easy to kind of look around and be like, "Oh my God, everything, set it all on fire and let's just be done!" [laughs] Especially right now, and I think that plugging in with folks and reading things and listening to things that are affirming and uplifting and do allow you to focus on the hopeful side of things are part of abolition. I'd like you to say something about that, but I have another part to that question, which is about self-care for those of us doing this work. That's something I spend a lot of time thinking about and talking about.*

Kaba: I always tell people, for me, hope doesn't preclude feeling sadness or frustration or anger or any other emotion that makes total sense. Hope isn't an emotion, you know? Hope is not optimism.

I think that for me, understanding that is really helpful in my practice around organizing. I believe that there's always a potential for transformation and for change. And that is in any direction, good or bad. The idea of hope being a discipline is something I heard from a nun many years ago who was talking about it in conjunction with making sure we were of the world and in the world. Living in the afterlife already in the present was kind of a form of escape, but it was really, really important for us to live in the world and be of the world. The hope that she was talking about was this grounded hope that was practiced every day, that people actually practiced all the time.

I bowed down to that. I heard that many years ago, and then I felt the sense of, "Oh my God. That speaks to me as a philosophy of living, that hope is a discipline and that we have to practice it every single day." Because in the world we live in, it's easy to feel a sense of hopelessness, that everything is all bad all the time, that nothing is going to change ever, that people are evil and bad at the bottom. It feels sometimes that it's being proven in various different ways, so I really get that. I understand why people feel that way. I just choose differently. I choose to think a different way, and I choose to act in a different way. I choose to trust people until they prove themselves untrustworthy.

Jim Wallace, who people know as a liberal Evangelical, who thinks about faith a lot and talks about faith a lot, he always talks about the fact that hope is really believing in spite of the evidence and watching the evidence change. And that, to me, makes total sense. I believe ultimately that we're going to win, because I believe there are more people who want justice, real justice, than there are those who are working against that.

And I don't take a short-term view. I take a long view, understanding full well that I'm just a tiny, little part of a story that already has a huge antecedent and has something that is going to come after that. I'm definitely not going to be even close to around for seeing the end of it. That also puts me in the right frame of mind: that my little friggin' thing I'm doing is actually pretty insignificant in world history, but if it's significant to one or two people, I feel good about that. If I'm making my stand in the world and that benefits my particular community of people, the people I designate as my community, and I see them benefiting by my labor, I feel good about that. That actually is enough for me.

Maybe I just have a different perspective. I talk to a lot of young organizers—people reach out to me a lot because I've been organizing for a long time—I'm always telling them—"Your timeline is not the timeline on which movements occur. Your timeline is incidental. Your timeline is only for yourself to mark your growth and your living." But that's a fraction of the living that's going to be done by the universe and that has already been done by the universe. When you understand that you're really insignificant in the grand scheme of things, then it's a freedom, in my opinion, to actually be able to do the work that's necessary as you see it and to contribute in the ways that you see fit.

And self-care is really tricky for me because I don't believe in the self in the way that people determine it here in this capitalist society that we live in. I don't believe in self-care: I believe in collective care, collectivizing our care, and thinking more about how we can help each other. How can we collectivize the care of children so that more people can feel like they can actually have their kids but also live in the world and contribute and participate in various different ways? How do we do that?

How do we collectivize care so that when we're sick and we're not feeling ourselves, we've got a crew of people who are not just our prayer warriors but our action warriors who are thinking through with us? Like, I'm just not going to be able to cook this week, and you have a whole bunch of folks there who are just putting a list together for you and bringing food every day that week, and you're doing the same for your community too.

I want that as the focus of how I do things, and that really comes from the fact that I grew up the daughter of returned migrants, African returned migrants. I don't see the world the way that people do here. I don't agree with it; I think capitalism is actually continuously alienating us from each other, but also even from ourselves, and I just don't subscribe. For me, it's too much, "Yeah, I'm going to go do yoga, and then I'm going to go and do some sit-ups and maybe I'll go . . . " You don't have to go anywhere to care for yourself. You can just care for yourself and your community in tandem, and that can actually be much more healthy for you, by the way. Because all this internalized reflection is not good for people. Yes, think about yourself, reflect on your practice, okay. But then you need to test it in the world; you've got to be with people. That's important. And I hate people! So I say that as somebody who actually is really antisocial.

[Wilson and Sonenstein laugh]

Kaba: And I say, "I hate people." I don't want to socialize in that kind of way, but I do want to be social with other folks as it relates to collectivizing care.

PART II

There Are No
Perfect Victims

Free Marissa and All Black People

In These Times, November 2014

"What if she goes to jail again? How will you feel?"

The questions bring me up short. My goddaughter hasn't previously expressed an interest in Marissa Alexander. She knows that I've been involved in a local defense committee to support Marissa in her struggle for freedom. But up to this point, she hasn't asked any questions. Her mother, however, tells me that Nina (not her real name) has been following my updates on social media.

I'm still considering how to respond, and I must have been silent for too long because Nina apologizes. "Forget about it, Auntie," she says. "I didn't mean to upset you."

It's interesting that she thinks I am upset. She knows that I have no faith in the US criminal legal system and perhaps assumes that I am pessimistic about Marissa's prospects in court. I tell her that while I have no faith in the criminal punishment system, I am hopeful for a legal victory in Marissa's case.

I say that while the system as a whole is unjust, in some individual cases legal victories can be achieved. I tell her that this is particularly true for defendants who have good legal representation and resources. Money makes a difference in securing legal victories. I explain that this is why I have worked so hard to fundraise for Marissa's legal defense.

"But how will you *feel* if she's convicted again, though?" Nina persists.

"I'll definitely be sad for her and her family," I respond.

"I think that you'll be a lot more than sad," she says.

Does sadness have levels? I guess so. I'm not sure what "more than sad" feels like, so I keep quiet.

A friend who has spent years supporting Marissa Alexander through the Free Marissa NOW National Mobilization Campaign recently confided that she was unable to contemplate another conviction for Marissa at her retrial in December. Many of us who've been supporting Marissa have been bracing ourselves. Each of us trying to cope as best we can. Over the past few weeks, I'd taken to asking comrades if they believed that Marissa would be free. Some answered affirmatively without hesitation, but they were in the minority. Most eyed me warily and slowly said that they were hopeful of an acquittal. I don't think that they believed what they were saying.

The US criminal punishment system cannot deliver any "justice." Marissa has already served over a thousand days in jail and prison. She spent another year under strict house arrest wearing an ankle monitor costing her family $105 every two weeks. Marissa fired a warning shot to ward off her abusive husband and no one was injured. For this, she was facing a sixty-year sentence if convicted in her retrial. True justice is not being arrested and taken away from her children, family, and friends. Justice is living a life free of domestic abuse. Justice is benefiting from state protection rather than suffering from state violence. Justice is having a self to defend in the first place.

Yesterday morning, I got news that Marissa had agreed to a plea deal. A couple of hours later, the news broke on social media. I saw a mix of people celebrating this outcome and others expressing their anger that Marissa was forced into a Faustian "choice." I got calls, texts, and emails from friends and family checking in on me. I appreciated everyone's concern, but I was unfortunately thrust into action when I heard that the grand jury in St. Louis would be announcing their indictment decision in the killing of Mike Brown later in the day. It was a mad rush to make arrangements to combine solidarity events since we already had one planned for Marissa yesterday evening.

The parallels between Marissa's unjust prosecution and imprisonment and Mike Brown's killing by law enforcement are evident to me. Yet I am well aware that for too many these are treated as distinct and separate occurrences. They are not. In fact, the logic of anti-Blackness and punishment connects both.

In the late nineteenth century, a remark was attributed to a southern police chief who suggested that there were three types of homicides: "If a nigger kills a white man, that's murder. If a white man kills a nigger, that's justifiable homicide. If a nigger kills a nigger, that's one less nigger."

The devaluing of Black life in this country has its roots in colonial America. In the book *Popular Justice: A History of Lynching in America*, Manfred Berg makes a convincing case that "the slave codes singled out Blacks for extremely cruel punishment, thus marking Black bodies as innately inferior." Berg argues: "Colonial slavery set clear patterns for future racial violence in America."

"Innately inferior" bodies can be debased, punished, and killed without consequence. The twist is that Black people have always been considered dangerous along with our disposability. Mike Brown's (disposable) body is a lethal weapon, and so he is justifiably threatening. Marissa's (disposable) body is deserving of abuse and is incapable of claiming a self worth defending. Mike Brown was described by his killer, Darren Wilson, as a "demon" and called an "it." The doctrine of preemptive killing and preventative captivity finds expression in the daily lives of all Black people in the United States. Black people are never "innocent." That language or concept doesn't apply. We are always guilty until proven something less than suspect or dangerous.

Marissa and Mike are inextricably linked. They can only be seen as the aggressors and are never the victims. Mike is painted as a super-subhuman, and Marissa is described as not seeming fearful. Black skin is a repellent to empathy, which makes it difficult to seek redress in courts of law and public opinion. If we can't generate empathy in others, then the humanity that is denied to us is always out of reach.

So, we combined our solidarity actions for Marissa and for Mike yesterday because we take it as a fact that all #BlackLivesMatter. Charlene Carruthers of BYP100 made this clear as she lifted up the name of Islan Nettles alongside those of Marissa and Mike.

I'm not naive, though. I know that our response to the grand jury non-indictment of Darren Wilson unfortunately stands apart from some of the others. I thought about some lines from one of my favorite poems "Sister Outsider" by Opal Palmer Adisa yesterday:

we
women Black
we

women Black
are always
outside
even when
we believe
we're in

Marissa, Cece, Islan, Monica, Tanesha, and many others are too often
outside of our discourse about interpersonal and state violence, and so
they are outside of our protests too. It's imperative that they be brought
inside and centered.

Marissa decided that she had had enough of living in the in-between.
Not behind the walls of the prison yet not quite outside. She made a decision for herself and her family to accelerate the possibility that she can
experience again the (unfree) freedom that all of us who live Black in the
United States have when we aren't formally caged. She should have been
able to demand total freedom, but this must feel like Everest. So she took
a plea that will ensure that she won't spend the rest of her natural life in a
cage. As Alisa Bierria of Free Marissa NOW said yesterday:

> The deal will help Marissa and her family avoid yet another very ex-
> pensive and emotionally exhausting trial that could have led to the
> devastating ruling of spending the rest of her life in prison. Marissa's
> children, family, and community need her to be free as soon as pos-
> sible. However, the absurdity in Marissa's case was always the fact
> that the courts punished and criminalized her for surviving domestic
> violence, for saving her own life. The mandatory minimum sentences
> of twenty years, and then sixty years, just made the state's prosecu-
> tion increasingly shocking. But we have always believed that forcing
> Marissa to serve even one day in prison represents a profound and
> systemic attack on Black women's right to exist and all women's right
> to self-defense.

When I've been tabling or facilitating teach-ins about Marissa,
people sometimes ask if I know her personally. I don't. I can read the
questions on their faces. "Why then are you talking about her case?
Why are you committed to her freedom?" I devoted so many hours to
raising awareness and funds for Marissa's legal defense because she is a
human being who has been unjustly targeted and is *still* fighting to get

free. I'm always on the freedom side. Marissa's unfreedom cages me.
Who will keep our sisters if not us?

> If I hadn't helped my sister
> They'd have put those chains on me!
> They tied her body to a tree and left her bleeding until we
> Cut her down and took her home
> As a daughter.
> —Niobeh Tsaba, "Song of a Sister's Freedom"

Yesterday, I stood in the freezing Chicago night with hundreds of
other people to show our solidarity with Marissa. In our own way, we
were cutting her down from the tree to take her home as a sister.

Until Marissa is free . . .

Not a Cardboard Cutout:
Cyntoia Brown and
the Framing of a Victim

with Brit Schulte

The Appeal, December 2017

The evening of August 6, 2004, sixteen-year-old Cyntoia Brown shot and killed Johnny Allen, a forty-three-year-old Nashville resident who picked her up for sex. It was an act of self-defense, she explained to police later; after Allen took her to his house, he showed Cyntoia multiple guns, including shotguns and rifles. Later in bed, as she described in court, he grabbed her violently by the genitals, his demeanor became threatening, and, fearing for her life, she took a gun out of her purse and shot him.

Though Cyntoia acted to protect herself from the violence of an adult client, Nashville prosecutors argued that she shot Allen as part of a robbery. Cyntoia was tried as an adult and was convicted of first-degree premeditated murder, first-degree felony murder, and "especially aggravated robbery" two years after her initial arrest on August 25, 2006. She is currently serving concurrent life sentences in Tennessee and will only be eligible for parole after serving fifty-one years in prison.

In late November, Cyntoia's case roared into the headlines again when celebrities like Rihanna, Kim Kardashian, and LeBron James shared details of her conviction on social media. Rihanna posted on Instagram: "Did we somehow change the definition of #JUSTICE along the way?? Something is horribly wrong when the system enables these rapists and the victim is thrown away for life! To each of you responsible for this child's sentence I hope to God you don't have children, because this could be your daughter being punished for punishing already!" Kim Kardashian shared on Twitter that she had reached out to her personal attorneys to ask about how to #FreeCyntoiaBrown.

It's unclear why Cyntoia's case has reemerged to capture the public's imagination thirteen years after her arrest. Charles Bone, one of Cyntoia's lawyers, told *Buzzfeed* that he didn't know why celebrities were now discovering Cyntoia's case, but that he welcomed the attention. "This issue, in general, is worthy of a lot of publicity," Bone said, "especially in the culture in which we live today." As petitions calling for Cyntoia's release and letters demanding clemency circulate online, it's worth considering the issues raised by Cyntoia's conviction and the renewed push to free her from prison.

Here's what has been established about her case in the court record: Cyntoia, who at the time of the incident was living in a room at a Nashville InTown Suites, said she went home with Allen because her pimp and boyfriend Garion McGlothen, nicknamed "Kut Throat," insisted that she needed to earn money. Kut Throat abused her physically and sexually throughout the approximately three-week period in which she lived with him.

Cyntoia herself was able to talk about the night of her attack and Allen's death in the 2011 PBS documentary *Me Facing Life: Cyntoia's Story*. Cyntoia explained that she was looking to get a ride to East Nashville to engage in street-based sex work when she met Allen, who was scouring a Sonic Drive-In parking lot for sex workers. Allen propositioned her and attempted to haggle her down from $200 to $100; they finally agreed upon $150.

Cyntoia characterized her survival strategies as survival sex work or teenage prostitution for an adult pimp. While she says that she was coerced into sex work by Kut Throat, Cyntoia never described herself as a child sex slave, a term that is now being used to characterize her experience by some advocates on social media. Such sensationalist language is reductionist and obscures the complexities inherent in the experiences of young people in the sex trade and street economies. It is more helpful to turn to young women in the sex trade themselves for a better understanding of the terms they use to describe their own experiences.

Shira Hassan has worked with girls involved in the sex trade and street economies as the former codirector of the now defunct Chicago-based Young Women's Empowerment Project. She defines the sex trade as "any way that girls are trading sex or sexuality, or forced to trade sex or sexuality, for anything like money, gifts, survival needs, documentation, places to stay, drugs."

Survival sex and involvement in the sex trade are often the only means for young people to provide for themselves when they leave home. This is especially true for youth of color and queer and trans youth, who have less access to resources and opportunities. The realities faced by most teenagers engaged in survival sex are shaped by unsafe homes and housing, lack of access to employment, affordable housing, health care including gender affirming health care, mental health resources, and by poverty, racism, queerphobia, and misogyny.

The street economy, Hassan explained, encompasses "anything that you do for cash that's not taxed. Whether that's hair braiding, whether that's selling CDs on the corner, something that you're gonna do that's gonna get you money that isn't reportable. Both of these methods are ways that girls have found to survive when they're street-based." Trafficking, on the other hand, refers to any form of labor—including, but not limited to, sexual labor—by force, fraud or coercion. It's true that there are young people who are trafficked and who experience extraordinary violence in the sex trade. But it is important not to assume that every young person who trades sex for money is trafficked, even if the law defines everyone under the age of eighteen who trades sex as trafficked, regardless of their actual experience. Doing so ignores the complexity of their experiences—and does a disservice to them by denying them any agency or self-determination, including to define their own experiences and demand their own solutions. Their lives should not be flattened in the service of perfect-victim narratives.

Cyntoia is not a cardboard cutout upon whom other adults can project their narratives of youth involvement in the sex trades. She is a young woman who has experienced horrible violence, but that is not all she is. She has her own story to tell, but by portraying her as a victim without agency some of Cyntoia's advocates make it more difficult for her story of self-defense, her fight to survive, and her resistance to

violence to be respected. We need to find a way to describe all of her realities—both as a survivor of violence with the right to defend herself,
and as a young woman who was doing her best to survive.

Will this renewed focus on Cyntoia serve to improve the lives of all
young people in the sex trade and street economies? Or will the current
attention and the framing of her as a victim of sex "slavery" or trafficking
serve to further marginalize them by silencing their voices and complexities in service of pursuing a perfect-victim narrative, one that Black
women are routinely excluded from?

The consequences for young women who don't fit the perfect-victim narrative are significant—both in terms of being harshly punished
for self-defense and being framed as "traffickers" themselves and then
threatened with long sentences under new laws ostensibly passed for
their own protection. Even if not subjected to punishment by what we
call the criminal legal system—because we believe there is no justice
in this system—any of the new trafficking laws passed at the state level
over the past decade may force them back into foster care and other
systems they have fled because of the harm they experienced. Or, these
laws may coerce them into "treatment" that does nothing to address the
conditions under which they entered the sex trade in the first place. If
they don't "comply" with what is expected of them as perfect victims,
then they, like many other survivors of violence, may find themselves
caged in a cell instead of receiving the support they need and deserve.
Prosecuting and incarcerating survivors of violence puts courts and
prisons in the same punitive role as their abusers, which compounds
and prolongs victims' experience of ongoing trauma and abuse.

The push to keep Cyntoia a child is also troubling. Since the recent surge of interest in her case, graphic artists have created images
of Brown with the pigtails she donned during her trial, when she was
sixteen, accompanied by the text, "Free Cyntoia." Another image of her
at a similar age has been appropriated into a meme, juxtaposed with
the rapist Brock Turner's mugshot, using her incorrect age and uncon-
firmed case circumstances. Other memes have claimed a "pedophile
sex trafficking ring" was responsible for the violence visited upon Cyntoia. Why are these images and memes being circulated? Is an adult,
twenty-nine-year-old Black woman an unsympathetic victim? If so

why? Acknowledging trauma and resilience are often ignored in favor of the driving desire by the media and public to support only a perfect victim. Perfect victims are submissive, not aggressive; they don't have histories of drug use or prior contact with the criminal legal system; and they are "innocent" and respectable.

The reality, however, is there are no perfect victims. Twenty-nine-year-old Cyntoia deserves to be free from prison and absolved of this "crime," no less than sixteen-year-young Cyntoia should have been.

Cyntoia's story, while tragic and unfair, is not exceptional. As we were writing this piece, Alisha Walker, another criminalized survivor, called us from Decatur Correctional Center, an Illinois prison where she has been incarcerated since March of this year (and, unless she is freed, will have to spend another ten years). "She's an amazing woman, so brave," Alisha said of Cyntoia's case. "Shit, she was sixteen? No one should be punished for enduring harm themselves. That girl was just doing what she had to do."

Alisha Walker was just nineteen years old when, in 2014, she was forced to defend herself and a friend from a violent client who demanded that they have unprotected sex with him and threatened them with rape and a knife. Alisha, like Cyntoia before her and so many before them, fought back. Her act of self-defense was met with the violence of a racist court system that branded her a manipulative criminal mastermind. Alisha and Cyntoia were both young Black women whose bodies were inscribed with inherent criminality and were, to some degree, presumed guilty until proven innocent. The judicial system as currently constituted would and could not have allowed them to be seen as innocent. Instead, Cyntoia's and Alisha's radical acts of self-love and preservation were criminalized by those with authority; each had the carceral weight of racism and whorephobia stacked against them.

Courts historically mete out punishment disproportionate to the acts of self-defense by Black women, femmes, and trans people. This criminalization of self-defense predates Cyntoia; we see this in the cases of survivors Lena Baker, Dessie Woods, and Rosa Lee Ingram, for example. It has continued long after Cyntoia's sentencing thirteen years ago. We see this same disproportionate punishment in the more recent cases of GiGi Thomas, CeCe McDonald, and Ky Peterson. And these are just the names and stories that we know; there are many others that never grab headlines or inspire social media or grassroots defense campaigns.

Let's #FreeCyntoiaBrown—not only from the cage she has unjustly been held in for the past thirteen years for fighting for her life, but also from narratives that take away her agency and police and control what it means to be a survivor of violence. And let's do the same for all young people in the sex trade, and all survivors of violence.

In the words of the Young Women's Empowerment Project, "Social justice for girls and young women in the sex trade means having the power to make all of the decisions about our own bodies and lives without policing, punishment, or violence. . . . We are not the problem—we are the solution."*

---

* Young Women's Empowerment Project, "Girls Do What They Have to Do to Survive: Illuminating Methods Used by Girls in the Sex Trade and Street Economy to Fight Back and Heal" (2009).

From "Me Too" to "All of Us": Organizing to End Sexual Violence without Prisons

Interview by Sarah Jaffe with Mariame Kaba and Shira Hassan
In *These Times*, January 2017

Sarah Jaffe: *Sexual harassment and sexual assault are in the news because of a powerful, famous man. I wanted to start off with a question for both of you, who have been doing this work for a while. Do you feel like the public conversation around these people—in the media, on social media, or wherever you are hearing it—has progressed at all? Does it look different right now from when you began doing this work?*

Mariame Kaba: The conversation is absolutely different from when I started doing work around sexual assault. I began doing anti–sexual assault work on my college campus. That was in the late 1980s and early 1990s. The focus at that point was on the question of date rape on campus, and the conversation revolved mostly around people drinking and then assaulting people.

I also came of age before social media. The conversation was very much limited to having talks with your friends. It wasn't this kind of generalized conversation that is not even really a conversation, which is more often a one-way harangue, a one-way rant, or just venting. It really wasn't like that. You had to talk to people you knew.

Beyond that, we were talking with folks in support-group settings, storytelling and divulging that you had been raped. It wasn't an environment of compulsory confession, where we were forced into disclosing that you were a survivor of sexual violence. It didn't feel like we had

41

to premise our conversations on disclosing our experiences before we could actually speak to this in real ways. I, yes indeed, am a survivor of sexual assault and violence, but it just felt different at that time. It felt somehow more intimate, and less tied to media and social media.

I don't know when the movie *The Accused* came out. I often see that movie in my trajectory of coming into my own and understanding sexual violence. That movie felt like a moment that made sexual violence connect much more with a larger media conversation. But maybe I am remembering that wrong.

Shira Hassan: I totally remember when that movie came out, and it really did change the conversation. Bless Jodie Foster. I think the conversation has definitely changed. We have the conversation much more publicly. It is a lot different from writing people's names on the bathroom walls, which is what we were doing in the 1990s. Facebook has become the bathroom wall, in a way. I think the way we have the conversation changes. Then, I think because it is a more democratized platform, to some degree, different people are in the conversation than used to be. I do think that, by and large, the people who are having the conversation are still the same, though.

I don't see this conversation happening in the same way about young people in the sex trade, for example. A lot of the young people I know are more street-based: the idea of sexual harassment is something that people are thinking about and angry about. Gwyneth Paltrow is not commenting on their experiences. She is commenting on actresses in Hollywood. I don't want to diminish or demean how important those experiences of violence are. At the same time, it is a certain kind of survivor and a certain kind of violence that we are all talking about. I think that part is the same.

Jaffe: *One of the things about this big public conversation is that, for me, it actually feels more overwhelming. What Mariame called this culture of compulsory confession feels smothering. It just feels like there is nothing we can do. You have been doing work around this for a while and dealing directly with survivors. How do you fight that feeling that this is never going to end?*

Hassan: There are stories that overwhelm me and stop me in my tracks. But they are also the stories of people I love, and there is a face to the story most of the time for me. The feeling of being overwhelmed is something that I counter with action and I counter with healing. This idea of healing justice, where speaking out is part of that healing—I feel connected to that as an action, not so much connected to that as a burden. I feel like it is a blessing to be among survivor stories. I don't actually feel overwhelmed by survivor stories. I feel overwhelmed by inaction around survivor stories.

Kaba: For me it is the difference between the question of asking what I can personally do versus what we can do. When I think of what I can do as an individual person, it feels more overwhelming. It is like, "Well, a lot of my friends are survivors. A lot of people I care for and love are survivors. I can't personally take responsibility for all of their lives and their pain, I can't take all of that on."

You can't also just take on everybody's joy either. When I think about it in that kind of individualistic way, it can feel overwhelming. But I have worked toward a collective idea of healing and a collective idea of action and organizing.

I don't think that the issue we have right now is that we have too many organizers. I think we have too few organizers, and that can also feel super debilitating when there is a lot of hand-wringing or a lot of outrage but without any direction. I think that can feel overwhelming. Since 1988, since I have been in this field, what has kept me going is that collectivity and seeking to actually understand and to heal and to be part of that healing process with other people.

Jaffe: *We end up with this story of one survivor who has to come forward and file charges with the police, and then this one perpetrator will be held accountable. But that doesn't work.*

Kaba: And it doesn't happen. I think that is another aspect of this for people who are counting on a criminal punishment response to this. I understand feeling completely depressed and debilitated, because that system doesn't actually know how to hold firm for survivors. It doesn't know how to transform harm that occurs. It is a system that most people don't access, and most survivors still never access for lots of reasons—because they don't want to, because they have been traumatized in the past by the system, because they don't want the person who harmed them necessarily caught up in the system. There are a million reasons. Because they don't want to be raked over the coals themselves. Because they try to solve problems in community. When people do access the system, they are screwed over by it, literally, in all different kinds of ways.

Hassan: Not only can't the system do it, but I think our belief that it can is part of why we feel so betrayed. Some of us have let go of that betrayal, because we have just stopped trying to get water from a stone. Frankly, the stone is being thrown at us. So we are now trying to build shelter from the stone, and talk to everyone who is coming inside the shelter about what we can do. That, for me, is perhaps why I feel less overwhelmed.

It isn't that I don't feel like, "Wow, we have an unbelievable amount to do," because I do feel like that. But I do feel like we have so many more things to try away from the system than with it. What we have begun to create is this shelter together, where we really can focus on who is inside this huddle and work with each person who is there in a more meaningful way to move forward.

Jaffe: *In the wake of the Weinstein revelations, one of the things that some people have been talking about is the whisper network. This is the way that women warn each other about certain men in their political circles or in their work circles. Yet these feel inadequate too—they are not particularly accountable for the people making accusations, which is less a problem than the fact that they just end up assuming that it is still our job to avoid perpetrators.*

Kaba: You can't force somebody into being accountable for things they do. That is not possible. People have to take accountability for things that they actually do wrong. They have to decide that this is wrong. They have to say, "This is wrong and I want to be part of making some sort of amends or repairing this or not doing it again." The question is: What in our culture allows people to do that? What are the structural things that exist? What in our culture encourages people who assault people and harm people to take responsibility? What I see is almost nothing. That means, for example, people continue to be rewarded when they do bad things to other people or take negative action against people.

We are in a situation where people try to argue over semantics. We don't have a sense that people are prepared to say, "There is a spectrum of sexual harm. Not everything is rape. Yet everything that feels like a violation is harm." We just don't have that within the larger culture that allows for people to feel like they can take responsibility and that they can be accountable.

The other thing is, we do have the threat that if you do admit that you do this, you might be caught up in the criminal punishment system. You might see the inside of a jail. So your inclination is to deny, deny, deny until the very end. There is just no incentive for you to come clean and be like, "I actually did this. Yes, I did rape this person. I did sexually assault them. I did harass them. I did molest them." We are in this adversarial model where you don't admit it, and the person who is actually being placed on trial is the survivor, to prove that you actually did this. So I understand, within that, why people feel like they have to whisper and why survivors then have to take on the weight of actually figuring out how to bring somebody to accountability. The incentive structure is set up this way.

Jaffe: *And, of course, not all survivors are women.*

Kaba: Exactly. This is, to me, the work that we have to do. We have to make community members understand what sexual harm looks like, what it feels like, why it is unacceptable. We have to make violence unthinkable in our culture. We have to make interpersonal violence unthinkable. That is the place that we have to work from if we are really going to transform this into something where it isn't the survivors or the victims who have to carry the load all the time.

Hassan: I want to add one thing: the history of where those lists come from. Those kinds of lists got started with people in the sex trade, in particular transgender women of color, who started creating bad date sheets. These were informal sheets, literally, that were written down and passed around through the community. We used to photocopy them, copy them down and hand them out with people's physical descriptions. The rest of the world looks at people in the sex trade as completely disposable, but we borrow their tools all the time when we feel disposable.

I want to be sure that we recognize the history and legacy of the tools that are being used, how they are being used, and why they are being used before we say that they are not working or important. Because the next thing just has to grow out of that. What is the next thing we are going to do with those lists? We went from the bathroom wall to Facebook. We went from photocopying the sheet with descriptions to passing it around online. We do have the power and capacity to think of "what next?" but we haven't quite yet. In part, it's because we don't have solidarity with each other, and we don't recognize that the spectrum of sexual violence is something that is happening to all of us. We live in rape culture, and all of this is going to keep happening to us until we can collectively figure out what we are doing here.

Kaba: As Shira mentioned early on, who are the survivors we are actually uplifting? Who are the people? What is sexual violence? When we put people in prisons and in jails, often we are sentencing them to judicial rape because we know they are going to be assaulted when they go inside. Yet we are still putting people in that environment to be assaulted. How are you going to be an anti-rape advocate or organizer and still be pressing for people to be put into rape factories?

We have to complicate this conversation around sexual violence and see all the different ways that it is used as a form of social control, across the board, with many different people from all different genders, all different races, and all different social locations. If we understand the problem in that way, we have a better shot at actually uprooting all of the conditions that lead to this and addressing all of the ways in which sexual violence reinforces other forms of violence. Our work over a couple of decades now has been devoted to complicating narratives that are too easy, these really simple narratives around perfect victims who are assaulted by evil monsters, and that is the end of the story. The "kill all rapists" conversation, which just kind of flattens what sexual violence really is, that doesn't take into consideration the spectrum of sexual violence, minimizes certain people's experiences and makes other people's experiences more valid. I want to press my concern about the perfect-victim narrative but also challenge the assumption that we all have the same experience because we have been raped, and we all think the same way about how to address it, and that for all of us being a rape survivor becomes your identity. We were raped. Something bad happened to us. We are trying to address that, but we are not taking on the survivor as a totalizing identity for everything we do in our lives and that matters.

I want more of those kinds of conversations to be happening in public, but somehow we can't have those. We can't have complicated conversations about sexual violence because then you are accused of rape apologia, or you are accused of coddling rapists. That is very, very limiting. It means that we are not going to be able to uproot and really solve the problem ultimately.

Hassan: I don't know what is going to happen with Mr. Weinstein, but I know that he has enough money to make what he wants to happen a possibility. The consequences that are going to happen to him, they may never measure up to the harm that he created. Yet we see wide-scale harm happening for people who may, ultimately, want to be accountable. Sexual violence is very nuanced, and the system that we have is not. Prison is as not feminist. That is one of Mariame's famous points. Prison isn't feminist, because it re-creates the same sexual violence and the same fear, the same kinds of oppression. It is the pin on the head of the racist and sexist system that we live in.

That does not mean, however, there should be no consequences. It means real consequences. Consequences that really matter. It means transforming the conditions that exist in the first place for this to even have happened. It is really critical for people to think about the difference between punishment and consequences. Punishment often is actually not the same as transformation. Even though it feels good to wear the "kill the rapists" T-shirt, that isn't the thing that is actually going to get us the world we want to live in.

Kaba: I also want to talk a little bit about what is hopeful about what is happening in the world around these issues. Shira and I just spent three and a half days in Chicago with fifty people from around the country, doing trainings and facilitating discussion and dialogue about how we do community accountability to address sexual harm and interpersonal violence. These folks came together from all around the country and took that much time out of their day, because we understand this as a moment of opportunity for something different. A lot of people are talking now, and there is much more awareness around the fact that the prison-industrial complex has churned communities and people through a meat grinder, devastating people. Yet people don't feel safer. People don't feel as though violence is "curbed" in any way.

We have to build up the skills of being able to ask questions like: What does it mean to actually center a survivor who is harmed? What does it mean to actually support people who have caused harm? What does it mean to take responsibility for saying, "We refuse in our community to condone when this happens?" One of the things that is so important is that harm causes wounds that necessitate healing. That is what so many people are looking for—a way to begin to heal. How are we going to create in our communities spaces that allow people real opportunity to heal?

Again, this will not necessarily be accomplished through compulsory confession in a public way. But how do we hold that people who have been harmed deserve an opportunity for that harm to be addressed in a real way? Often, that is all people want, a real acknowledgement that "I was hurt. Somebody did it. I want them to know that they did it. I want to see that they have some remorse for having done it, and I want them to start a process by which they will ensure to themselves, at least, and be accountable to their community, for not doing it again. That is what I am trying to get as a survivor." I think there is hope in that.

Black Women
Punished for Self-Defense
Must Be Freed from Their Cages

The Guardian, January 2019

On June 23, 1855, after enduring five years of sexual violence, Celia, a nineteen-year-old Missouri enslaved woman, killed her master, Robert Newsom. Newsom was a sixty-year-old widower who had purchased Celia when she was fourteen. On the day of her purchase, he raped her on the way to his farm. Sexual control of enslaved women by white owners was critical to the perpetuation of slavery, and these owners relied on routine sexual abuse as much as they did other forms of brutality.

By the time she killed Newsom, Celia already had two of his children and was pregnant with a third. She had started a relationship with one of Newsom's male slaves, George, who insisted that she end her sexual "relationship" with Newsom if they were going to continue theirs.

Celia approached Newsom's daughters and implored them to ask their father to end the sexual assaults. But no one could protect her, so she confronted Newsom herself when he came to force yet another unwanted sexual encounter. She clubbed him to death, then burned his body in her fireplace.

Her court-appointed lawyers suggested that a Missouri law permitting a woman to use deadly force to defend herself against sexual advances be extended to enslaved as well as free women. Despite their vigorous defense, the court disagreed: it found that Celia was property, not a person. But, while Celia was not considered a person under the law and could therefore not be raped, she did have enough agency to be judged a murderess and punished for her act of resistance. She was

49

found guilty of murder and sentenced to death by hanging. After an appeal of the case failed, Celia was hanged on December 21, 1855.

Black women have always been vulnerable to violence in this country and have long been judged as having "no selves to defend"—a term I devised and named an anthology on the subject after. When Ida B. Wells began her anti-lynching and anti-rape campaigns a few decades after Celia was hanged, in the late nineteenth century, she was determined to expose the myths that Black men were rapists and that Black women could not be raped. Wells insisted that Black women were entitled to state protection—and the recourse of self-defense—as a right of citizenship. In 2018, this right still proves elusive.

What has changed since Celia's time? Ask Marissa Alexander. In late January 2017, Alexander was freed from the shackles of her ankle monitor after two years of house arrest and three years of incarceration. Her freedom was secured through good lawyering and a national participatory legal defense organizing campaign. Alexander's tortuous journey through the criminal punishment system began in 2010, when she was confronted by her estranged husband in her home after having just given birth to her third child, a little girl, nine days earlier. Alexander used a gun that she was licensed to own and fired a single warning shot into the air to ward off her abusive husband, who admitted in a subsequent deposition to having abused every woman he had ever been partnered with (except for one).

For this, a jury found her guilty of aggravated assault with a deadly weapon following a twelve-minute deliberation. It was that deadly weapon charge that prosecutors used to recommend that Marissa be sentenced under Florida's 10-20-life law to a mandatory minimum sentence of 20 years. The judge, who had previously ruled that Marissa was ineligible to invoke the Stand Your Ground defense because she didn't appear afraid, said that his hands were tied by the law and ratified the 20-year sentence.

While self-defense laws are interpreted generously when applied to white men who feel threatened by men of color, they are applied very narrowly to women and gender nonconforming people, and particularly women and gender nonconforming people of color trying to protect themselves in domestic violence and sexual assault cases.

Black women have been excluded from definitions of "respectable" or "proper" womanhood, sexuality, and beauty, influencing how their right to bodily autonomy—and agency—is viewed.

In 2017, there were 219,000 women in US prisons and jails, most of them poor and of color. In 2014, according to the Sentencing Project, Black non-Hispanic females had an imprisonment rate over twice that of white non-Hispanic females.

Sociologist Beth Richie has suggested that a key to responding to women in conflict with the law is understanding their status as crime victims. Multiple studies indicate that between 71 percent and 95 percent of incarcerated women have experienced physical violence from an intimate partner. In addition, many have experienced multiple forms of physical and sexual abuse in childhood and as adults. This reality has been termed the abuse-to-prison pipeline.

These numbers are high because survivors are systematically punished for taking action to protect themselves and their children while living in unstable and dangerous conditions. Survivors are criminalized for self-defense, failing to control abusers' violence, migration, removing their children from situations of abuse, being coerced into criminalized activity, and securing resources needed to live day-to-day while suffering economic abuse.

Three years ago, I cofounded an organization called Survived & Punished. Our work focuses on freeing criminalized survivors of gender-based violence. Too many women and gender nonconforming people are in prison for defending themselves against their abusers, and we are demanding that governors Jerry Brown and Andrew Cuomo use their clemency powers to free these survivors from their cages. As Dr. Alisa Bierria, a cofounder of S&P, suggests: "Our political strategies must recognize that racialized gender violence and state violence are not isolated or oppositional, but integral to each other." We are determined to ensure that more people understand these connections.

On December 6, the Tennessee Supreme Court issued its decision stating that Cyntoia Brown, who was sentenced to life in prison at the age of sixteen for killing a man in self-defense who had picked her up for sex, must serve at least fifty-one years before becoming eligible for parole. People across the US were once again outraged as her case returned to public attention, and some have been moved to demand that the governor, Bill Haslam, commute her sentence before he leaves office on January 19, 2019. The governor is said to be considering clemency in her case, which is, unfortunately, not an exceptional one. There are thousands of Cyntoia Browns unjustly locked in cages in every state. We have to address the systemic and cultural issues that contribute to the criminalization of survival as we work to #FreeCyntoiaBrown and all of the others currently behind bars. One hundred sixty-five years ago Celia was killed for defending her bodily autonomy. Cyntoia Brown shouldn't die in prison for doing the same.*

---

* After years of resistance from Cyntoia Brown—and from organizations, activists, and celebrities demanding her release—on January 7, 2019, the Tennessee governor did indeed grant her full clemency. Cyntoia Brown-Long wrote and published her autobiography in late 2019. See *Free Cyntoia: My Search for Redemption in the American Prison System*, by Cyntoia Brown-Long with Bethany Mauger.

PART III

The State Can't Give Us Transformative Justice

Whether Darren Wilson Is Indicted or Not, the Entire System Is Guilty

In These Times, November 2014

Everyone I know is on edge. Will a grand jury in St. Louis indict or not?

On one hand, how will residents of Ferguson react if (as many expect) the grand jury advises against an indictment of Darren Wilson, the officer who killed Mike Brown?

What will be the response of the St. Louis and Ferguson police?

Photos of MRAPs (Mine-Resistant Ambush Protected police vehicles) and boarded up businesses proliferate on social media. Articles suggest that St. Louis police have recently stockpiled riot gear and military grade weapons. It's war, but that's not new. Everyone is holding their breath.

On the other hand, what's next if the grand jury does decide that Wilson should stand trial? So much psychic, emotional, and spiritual energy is focused on a successful indictment. I imagine the sighs of relief. I anticipate the countless social media posts crying out, "Justice!" I imagine that many exhausted protesters will decide that their work is done. I fear a return to our seductive slumber and to complacency.

I'm not invested in indicting Darren Wilson, though I understand its (symbolic) import to many people, especially Mike Brown's family and friends. Vincent Warren of the Center on Constitutional Rights speaks for many, I think, when he writes:

> Without accountability, there can be no rule of law. If Wilson is not indicted, or is under-indicted, the clear message is that it is open season on people of color, that St. Louis has declared that Darren Wilson is not a criminal but that the people who live under the thumbs

of the Darren Wilsons of this country are. It would say to the cry that "Black lives matter" that, no, in fact, they do not.

I understand the sentiment that Warren expresses. Yet I don't believe that an indictment of Wilson would be evidence that Black lives do in fact matter to anyone other than Black people. Nor do I think his indictment would mean that it was no longer open season on people of color in this country. If we are to take seriously that oppressive policing is not a problem of individual "bad apple" cops, then it must follow that a singular indictment will have little to no impact on ending police violence.

As I type, I can already feel the impatience and frustration of some who will read these words.

It feels blasphemous to suggest that one is disinvested from the outcome of the grand jury deliberations. "Don't you care about accountability for harm caused?" some will ask. "What about justice?" others will accuse. My response is always the same: I am not against indicting killer cops. I just know that indictments won't and can't end oppressive policing, which is rooted in anti-Blackness, social control, and containment. Policing is derivative of a broader social justice. It's impossible for non-oppressive policing to exist in a fundamentally oppressive and unjust society. The truth is that, as the authors of *Struggle for Justice* wrote in 1971, "without a radical change in our values and a drastic restructuring of our social and economic institutions," we can only achieve modest reforms of the criminal punishment system (including policing).

The pattern after police killings is all too familiar. Person X is shot, and killed. Person X is usually Black (or less frequently brown). Community members (sometimes) take to the streets in protest. They are (sometimes) brutally suppressed. The press calls for investigations. Advocates call for reforms suggesting that the current practices and systems are "broken" and/or unjust. There is a (racist) backlash by people who support the police. A very few people whisper that the essential nature of policing is oppressive and is not susceptible to any reforms, thus only abolition is realistic. These people are considered heretics by most. I've spent years participating in one way or another in this cycle.

Knowing all of this, what can and should we do to end oppressive policing? We have to take various actions in the short, medium, and long term. We have to act at the individual, community, institutional, and societal levels. For my own part, I start by never calling the cops. I hope more people will join me in that practice. It demands that we feel for the edge of our imaginations to stop relying on the police. It takes practice to do this. As such, we need popular education within our communities about alternatives to policing.

I vocally and actively oppose any calls for increased police presence as a response to harm in my community and in my city. At budget time, I pay attention to how much money is allocated to law enforcement. I press my local elected officials to oppose any increases in that amount and to instead advocate for a *decrease* in the police department's budget. I support campaigns for reparations to police torture and violence victims. I support elected civilian police accountability councils and boards (knowing full well that they are band-aids). I believe that we need grassroots organizations in every town and city that document and publicize the cases of people who have suffered from police violence. These organizations should use all levers of power to seek redress for those victims and their families.

I list these actions with the understanding that together they aren't enough to end oppressive policing. They will lessen the harm to be sure, but only building power among those most marginalized in society holds the possibility of radical transformation. And that's an endless quest for justice. That's a struggle rather than a goal. Only movements can build power. We need a movement for transformative justice.

To the young people who have taken to the streets across the country and are agitating for some "justice" in this moment, I hope that you don't invest too deeply in the Ferguson indictment decision. Don't let a non-indictment crush your spirit and steal your hope. Hope is a discipline. And, frankly, the actions you have taken and are taking inspire so many daily.

On the other hand, a decision to indict Darren Wilson isn't a victory for justice or an end. As I've already said, an indictment won't end police violence or prevent the death of another Mike Brown or Rekia Boyd or Dominique Franklin. We must organize with those most impacted by oppression, while also making room for others who want to join the struggle too, as comrades. As Kwame Ture often said: "We need each other. We have to have each other for our survival." Take this admonition seriously. We should use the occasion of the indictment announcement to gather and to continue to build power together. This is how we will win.

The Sentencing of Larry Nassar Was Not "Transformative Justice." Here's Why.

with Kelly Hayes
The Appeal, February 2018

For those of us who believe our "justice" system must be transformed, moments such as this one are tests of conviction.

On January 24, 2018, Larry Gerard Nassar, the former national team doctor of USA Gymnastics, was sentenced to 40 to 175 years in prison for the sexual assault of minors. The sentence was handed down with biting words from Judge Rosemarie Aquilina, after a week of intense and moving presentencing statements from Nassar's victims. Aquilina noted that if the Constitution did not forbid cruel and unusual punishment, she might have sentenced him to be made a victim of sexual violence. She settled for an unsurvivable prison sentence, saying, to great public applause, "I just signed your death warrant."

Amid our society's current cultural upheaval around sexual violence, Aquilina struck a chord with many survivors who want and need to believe that justice under this system is possible. By offering the mic to survivors and by aiming violent, vindictive language at a widely loathed defendant, Aquilina has been rewarded with the status of instant icon.

Unsurprisingly, she is also reportedly considering a run for the Michigan Supreme Court. The case launched numerous think pieces, including a misguided, misinformed praisesong in the *Atlantic* titled, "The Transformative Justice of Judge Aquilina," by Sophie Gilbert.

Gilbert's article highlights how this moment challenges those committed to transforming our carceral system—including people like us, who are committed to justice for survivors of sexual assault and who also believe that prisons are the wrong answer to violence and should be abolished. We decry the system and advocate for change that is long overdue. Yet when that system ensnares people we loathe, we may feel a sense of satisfaction. When we see defendants as symbols of what we most fear and that which we most greatly despise we are confronted with a true test of our belief that no justice can be done under this system.

Yet like all tests of faith, this moment calls on us to recommit ourselves to true transformative justice. And to do that, we must remind ourselves what transformative justice is, and why it looks nothing like the civil death that Aquilina delivered last month.

Transformative justice is not a flowery phrase for a court proceeding that delivers an outcome we like. It is a community process developed by anti-violence activists of color, in particular, who wanted to create responses to violence that do what criminal punishment systems fail to do: build support and more safety for the person harmed, figure out how the broader context was set up for this harm to happen, and how that context can be changed so that this harm is less likely to happen again. It is time-consuming and difficult work done by organizations like Generation 5, Creative Interventions, and the Bay Area Transformative Justice Collective. It is not grounded in punitive justice, and it actually requires us to challenge our punitive impulses, while prioritizing healing, repair, and accountability.

A truly transformative justice would mean that a single survivor coming forward to tell their tale of harm years ago would actually have been believed (the first time). We would immediately focus on addressing the harms perpetrated, centering on the concerns and experiences of the person who was harmed. Next, we would also focus on the person responsible for the harm—but without disregarding their humanity. This means we have to acknowledge the reality that often it is hurt people who hurt other people. Understanding that harm originates from situations dominated by stress, scarcity, and oppression, one way to prevent violence is to make sure that people have support to get the things they need. We must also create a culture that enables people to actually take accountability for violence and harm. The criminal punishment system promises accountability for violence, but we know that in actuality it is a form of targeted violence against poor people, people with disabilities, and people of color, and doesn't reduce violence in our society.

Real accountability calls us to respond to harm that occurs because the person responsible was struggling with mental illness by providing high-quality treatment. If violence emerged because of poverty and desperation, then creating survivable conditions might prevent future harm. If violence originated because of unexamined misogyny or sexism learned in the family or broader culture, a community process that invites the person responsible to examine that would be more likely to lead to a positive outcome than incarceration in a cell, where the person is likely to experience more violence.

Finally, in a truly transformative model of justice, we would not allow those harms to be shielded by powerful people or institutions. We would insist on focusing not just on individuals but also the institutions and structures that perpetuate, foster, and maintain interpersonal violence. In Nassar's case, this would include the administrators at Michigan State University and USA Gymnastics who ignored initial disclosures of sexual assault and took no actions to stop his violent behavior. Judge Aquilina's ruling accomplished none of these aims.

But, some say, even if the system itself is unjust, it can sometimes deliver justice—and we ought to recognize that justice when it comes. Let us be clear: our punishment system, which is grounded in genocide and slavery and which has continued to replicate the functions and themes of those atrocities, can never be made just. Prisons are an iteration of structural racism in the United States, which allows some people to be treated as less than human and therefore reasonably subject to all manner of exploitation, torture, and abuse. This is the legacy of anti-Blackness in the United States. Even when the system ensnares a non-Black person, the prison-industrial complex remains a structurally anti-Black apparatus, firmly rooted in the United States' ongoing reliance on the financial exploitation and social control of Black people. This can be seen in persistent disparities at all levels of the criminal legal system, from arrest through imprisonment.

Even if we firmly believe Nassar's sentence unjust, we may ask ourselves: Should we just sit by as the public applauds Nassar's sentence? Who wants to be considered an apologist for a serial rapist? After all, the reality is that most people who rape will never go on trial, let alone be convicted and sentenced to prison. So we wonder if we should just keep quiet and let the system "work" this time by imposing a draconian sentence.

But, perhaps above all, we may fear the questions we will be asked if we stand up against Nassar's sentence. What will we say when people who are already hostile to transformative justice aggressively demand a "solution" for addressing Nassar's abhorrent violent actions? "What's your alternative to a death sentence for someone who commits acts as heinous as Nassar's?" some will spit out derisively, as if the onus to create a safer society falls on the shoulders of single individuals rather than being a collective project decided together in community. One might be tempted to throw one's hands in the air and say, "You know what, the devil you know is better than the devil you don't." In other words, we remain stuck with the ineffective prison system as the remedy when sexual violence, for example, is perpetrated. This is not viable in our opinion. We must depart from the crowd that applauds the signing of "death warrants." Now, more than ever, we must call people toward a new vision of justice.

Granted, our vision is incomplete. There is no road map for justice, because under this system we have never seen it. But the current system has been thoroughly mapped, and it has already failed. While we all harbor fears about what it means for "dangerous people" to walk among us, we know in truth that such people have never ceased to walk among us, and that the purpose of the carceral system has never been to sort the "good" from the "bad."

We must also acknowledge that we simply do not know, and cannot know, what the occurrence, prevention, or resolution of harm could look like in our society under more just conditions. So long as the structures that instill desperation are maintained, some people will be shaped by desperation. And so long as we perpetuate mass criminalization—a security blanket with all the substance of "The Emperor's New Clothes"— we will not know what it would look like to live differently. If our rage and disgust can prompt us to endorse the violence of the carceral state, how can we expect to reach those who are skeptical of our view?

Transformative justice is comprised of creative and dynamic experiments happening across the world. It is also a revival of tools that were taken from us by a society that did not trust our ability to resolve harm without brutality. As educator and organizer James Kilgore has written, "Pre-1824 tribal courts embodied a restorative approach that greatly differed from the punitive, adversarial system of the United States." Deeming Native justice insufficiently punitive, and therefore uncivilized, the federal government assumed jurisdiction over all violations of the Major Crimes Act on Native reservations. The results, for Native people, have been devastating, as difficult conditions on reservations easily facilitate the criminalization of Native people, fueling high rates of incarceration.

That doesn't mean all hope is lost. Efforts like the Hollow Water First Nations Community Holistic Healing Circle, a community justice initiative geared toward reconciliation, illustrate that reclamation is possible. By establishing a healing justice practice grounded in Anishinaabe teachings, the Hollow Water community has developed a means to interrupt cycles of intra-community abuse and incarceration.

But as with so many justice infrastructures lost to colonial violence, we are not simply talking about the need to dismantle a larger system. We are talking about a process of construction and creativity, for all peoples whose systems of justice were upended or eradicated by the American political project. Neutralizing perceived threats, in an endless game of legal whack-a-mole, is not a path to safety. To create safer environments, people and circumstances must be transformed. We cannot discuss policing, prosecutions, judges, or prisons system without acknowledging the prison system as a mechanism of social death and exploitation.

When you say, "What would we do without prisons?" what you are really saying is: "What would we do without civil death, exploitation, and state-sanctioned violence?" That is an old question and the answer remains the same: whatever it takes to build a society that does not continuously rearrange the trappings of annihilation and bondage while calling itself "free." To know freedom or safety, and to make peace with our own fears, passive punishments must be replaced with active amends and accountability. Transformation is possible, but it will not be televised, and it will not be facilitated by the likes of Judge Rosemarie Aquilina.

We Want More Justice
for Breonna Taylor than the System
That Killed Her Can Deliver

with Andrea J. Ritchie

Essence, July 2020

Calls for arrests of the officers who killed Breonna Taylor are intensifying daily—Breonna's family, community, celebrities, social media, Black women, and allies across the United States are demanding equal justice for our sister slain by police. Many of these calls point to the arrests of officers who killed George Floyd and Rayshard Brooks days and weeks after their deaths, compared to the fact that there have been no arrests in Breonna's case more than one hundred days after she was killed as she slept in her bed in her home. One officer, Brett Hankison, has been fired; the other two remain on administrative leave. Both the FBI and a special Kentucky prosecutor are investigating Breonna's killing and whether charges can be brought against the officers.

We fully support demands for accountability for Breonna's death, and her family and loved ones' quest for justice. When agents of the state act violently against an individual and, in this case, callously and negligently take their life, there is no doubt that collective responses are absolutely warranted and essential. Collective responses can include uprisings, demands that the officers involved be fired and never allowed to serve in positions of power again, community campaigns to defund the police, and calls for compensation, healing, and repair for people harmed or families left behind. Calls for prosecution and imprisonment are just one of many possible collective responses to a clear injustice. Of course, individuals, families, and communities, including

Breonna's, are entitled to decide on their own paths for justice—including seeking justice in courts and criminal punishment.

As prison-industrial complex abolitionists, we want far more than what the system that killed Breonna Taylor can offer—because the system that killed her is not set up to provide justice for her family and loved ones. Experience shows that officers who harm are rarely arrested by the departments that employ them, and prosecutions and convictions are even more unlikely.

Since 2005 there have only been 110 prosecutions of police officers who shot people, while police have killed 1,000 people a year on average since 2014. There were convictions in less than forty-two cases, usually on lesser charges. Even when convicted, police officers' sentences—such as the two-year sentence handed down to Johannes Mesherle for killing Oscar Grant by shooting him point-blank in the back of the head on a subway platform as he lay on the ground, the three-year sentence for former Chicago Police Commander Jon Burge, who tortured confessions from over one hundred Black men and women, or the seven-year sentence Jason Van Dyke is currently serving for murdering Laquan McDonald—rarely bring satisfaction or healing to families and harmed communities.

The number of prosecutions of police officers has not increased in spite of consistent uprisings and attention to police violence over the past decade—because the law ultimately protects them. The officers who killed Breonna Taylor will claim self-defense because a confused, half-asleep person defending his home and his fiancée against what he reasonably believed to be a home invasion fired shots. And, even if they are arrested and brought to trial, if past experience is any indicator, the law will once again provide them with cover for killing another Black person. Meanwhile, countless Black women and trans people who act in self-defense when police fail to protect them languish in prison, denied the right to assert self-defense because our legal systems deems that they have no legitimate selves to defend, while consistently legitimizing the use of deadly force by officers who "reasonably" believe their lives are in danger, no matter how flimsy or rooted in deeply entrenched criminalizing narratives about Black people this belief might be.

Why are we asking the police to stop being the police over and over again? Ultimately, calls for collective responses rooted in arrests and prosecution are likely to lead to dead ends and deep disappointments. But even if successful, the arrest, conviction, and sentencing of individual cops represent an exception to the rule: the rule is impunity. Focusing on arrests leaves the whole system intact. As the popular chant goes, "Indict, convict, send the killer cops to jail, *the whole damn system is guilty as hell.*" The answer to why calls for arrests and prosecutions are unlikely to bear fruit, or bring about fundamental change to prevent future killings, is in the second half of the chant—which highlights the fundamental flaw in the demand reflected in the first half. We want to direct our energies toward collective strategies that are more likely to be successful in delivering healing and transformation and to prevent future harms. Families and communities deserve more than heartbreak over and over again each time the system declines to hold itself accountable.

Beyond strategic assessments of what is most likely to bring justice, ultimately we must choose to support collective responses that align with our values. Demands for arrests and prosecutions of killer cops are inconsistent with demands to #DefundPolice because they have proven to be sources of violence not safety. We can't claim the system must be dismantled because it is a danger to Black lives and at the same time legitimize it by turning to it for justice. As Angela Y. Davis points out, "we have to be consistent" in our analysis and not respond to violence in a way that compounds it. We need to use our radical imaginations to come up with new structures of accountability beyond the system we are working to dismantle.

This is neither a popular nor easy position to take. It's really, really hard. People who have been or seen their loved ones arrested, prosecuted, incarcerated, and killed for the slightest infraction—or none at all—want the system to act fairly by arresting, prosecuting, and incarcerating those who harm and kill us. People who have consistently been denied protection under the law desperately want the law to live up to its promises. There are ways to support families calling for arrests without legitimizing the system, including by meeting material needs, providing safety for families and communities, and working to disempower police.

Turning away from systems of policing and punishment doesn't mean turning away from accountability. It just means we stop setting the value of a life by how much time another person does in a cage for violating or taking it—particularly when the criminal punishment system has consistently made clear whose lives it will value and whose lives it will cage.

We want to invite a broader and deeper conception of justice for Breonna Taylor and other survivors and family members harmed by police violence—one rooted in reparations, modeled on Chicago's recent successful struggle for reparations for survivors and families of people tortured by former Chicago police commander Jon Burge. The reparations framework outlines five elements—repair, restoration, acknowledgment, cessation, and nonrepetition.

Under this framework, there is no question Breonna's family is entitled to accountability—including immediate termination of the officers involved in her killing, and banning them from any future position that would allow them to carry a weapon or hold a position of power that can be abused in the way they abused it in Breonna's case. They are also entitled to a process through which the officers must hear and be accountable to their pain, know the full value of the life they took, and make amends to our collective satisfaction. Breonna's family is entitled to repair—compensation for their pain and suffering, without the necessity of having to endure lengthy litigation during which their loved one's reputation, history, associations, character will be assailed, without having to look over and over at an incident report that states that no one was injured when their daughter and sister bled out in her bed in a hail of bullets, and without having to pay extensive litigation costs and undergo additional suffering through the process. They are also entitled to restoration and healing services.

Under a reparations framework, Breonna's family—and all of us—are also entitled to more than an individualized response to what is a systemic problem. We are entitled to immediate cessation of the actions that caused her death—no-knock warrants, to be sure, but also short-knock warrants and dangerous drug raids in all their forms. And all of us are entitled to nonrepetition, an end to the conditions that produced her death, including an end to the drug war that killed her, and the forces of gentrification that brought police into her neighborhood. It is long past time for an approach to drug use that saves lives instead of ending them—whether in a raid or in a cell—and a reckoning with the ways in which economic policies are driving deadly policing practices.

The Movement for Black Lives recently introduced the BREATHE Act, which enshrines demands of the Vision for Black Lives 2020 and calls for reparations for survivors of police violence—and the families of those who did not survive and for people impacted by the drug war—both of which would offer far more than prosecutions in Breonna's case. The M4BL Reparations Now toolkit offers an understanding of how these demands were actualized in Chicago, and how they fit into larger calls for reparations for the long legacy and continuing impacts of chattel slavery that produced not only Breonna's death but also that of George Floyd, Tony McDade, Remmie Fells, Breonna Hill, Rayshard Brooks, Elijah McClain, Brayla Stone, and so many more.

The Louisville City Council recently announced a resolution calling for an investigation into the mayor's administration and the events leading up to Breonna's killing, as well as police responses to the protests calling for justice in her case. This process could serve as a first step to a more comprehensive, reparations-based approach to justice for Breonna.

Breonna, and all of us, deserve so much more than arrests and prosecutions of individual officers can offer. We are demanding a bold and expansive version of justice in her name.

PART IV

Making Demands: Reforms for and against Abolition

Police "Reforms"
You Should Always Oppose

Truthout, December 2014

Here is a simple guide for evaluating any suggested reforms of US policing in this historic moment:

1) Are the proposed reforms allocating more money to the police? If yes, then you should oppose them.

2) Are the proposed reforms advocating for *more* police and policing (under euphemistic terms like "community policing" run out of regular police districts)? If yes, then you should oppose them.

3) Are the proposed reforms primarily technology-focused? If yes, then you should oppose them, because it means more money to the police. Said technology is more likely to be turned against the public than it is to be used against cops. Police violence won't end through technological advances (no matter what someone is selling you).

4) Are the proposed reforms focused on individual dialogues with individual cops? And will these "dialogues" be funded with tax dollars? I am never against dialogue. It's good to talk with people. These conversations, however, should not be funded by taxpayer money. That money is better spent elsewhere.

5) Additionally, violence is endemic to US policing itself. There are some nice individual people who work in police departments. I've met some of them. But individual dialogue projects reinforce the "bad apples" theory of oppressive policing. This is not a problem of

individually terrible officers; rather it is a problem of a corrupt and oppressive policing system built on controlling and managing the marginalized while protecting property.

What reforms should you support (in the interim), then?

1) Proposals and legislation to offer reparations to victims of police violence and their families.

2) Proposals and legislation to decrease and redirect policing and prison funds to other social goods.

3) Proposals and legislation for (elected) independent civilian police accountability boards with power to investigate, discipline, fire police officers and administrators (*with some serious caveats*).*

4) Proposals and legislation to disarm the police.

5) Proposals to simplify the process of dissolving existing police departments.

6) Proposals and legislation for data transparency (stops, arrests, budgeting, weapons, etc.).

7) Ultimately, the only way that we will address oppressive policing is to abolish the police. Therefore, all of the "reforms" that focus on strengthening the police or "morphing" policing into something more invisible but still as deadly should be opposed.

---

* See Beth Richie, Dylan Rodríguez, Mariame Kaba, Melissa Burch, Rachel Herzing and Shana Agid, "Problems with Community Control of Police and Proposals for Alternatives," Critical Resistance, https://bit.ly/CRBProblems.

A People's History of Prisons
in the United States

Interview by Jeremy Scahill

Intercepted, May 2017

Jeremy Scahill: *Now, you refer to yourself as an abolitionist. What do you mean by that?*

Mariame Kaba: Abolition for me is a long-term project and a practice around creating the conditions that would allow for the dismantling of prisons, policing, and surveillance and the creation of new institutions that actually work to keep us safe and are not fundamentally oppressive. What you need to make those conditions happen, you have to be for addressing environmental issues, you have to be for making sure people have a living wage economically. I know for me it's important to be anticapitalist.

Scahill: *For people who don't have a loved one that's been to prison, haven't been to prison themselves, just view prison as a place where people who commit crimes go, set a context for people of the institution of imprisonment in the United States and what that looks like.*

Kaba: Prison itself is a reform. I think that's something that most people don't think about. Prisons haven't always existed. They came into being, especially in the United States, because people were reacting against capital punishment and corporal punishment, which were seen at the time, particularly by Quakers, as incredibly inhumane. Initially the reform was not meant to be a brutalizing thing, but isolation itself is actually brutal. Over the years, prisons have been spaces where we've sent the people we don't like, or the people we want to manage and control socially.

Early before the Civil War, most people who were locked up were not actually Black people, because almost every Black person in the country was enslaved. Immediately after emancipation, all of a sudden, the literal complexion of prisons changed, and Black people became hyper-targets of that system as we created new laws like the Black Codes. The convict lease system comes into being as a way to continue to exploit the labor of the people who are now newly free.

The reason to talk about that history is to demystify how and why people ended up behind bars initially. It wasn't really about crime; it was about a perception that Black people were inherently criminal, that Black people couldn't manage freedom. That was the story that got told, and prison became a site for continuing to control Blackness.

In the late 1960s, violent crimes are rising at the same time as the Black Power movement is expanding, and these two things are being brought together.

Between 1825 until the late 1960s, the prison population is stable and pretty low. In the late 1960s you've got all these scholars and activists talking about the end of prison. People are talking about the prison as being over. You have to think about how the United States went from the end of prison to, all of a sudden, the largest jailer in the whole world. And that's because of a set of bipartisan policies, but really takes off with Lyndon B. Johnson. Johnson wants to fight the war on poverty, and he gives in on creating a war on crime arm of the war on poverty. And what do the Republicans do, which they always do so well? They defund the poverty angle and keep the war on crime.

Jeremy Scahill: *What was the motivation, in your assessment, of these politicians, both Democrats and Republicans?*

Mariame Kaba: It was the "riots." It was the images of those young Black people, in Harlem in 1964 and in Watts in 1965. In all these places where there were "urban disorder and urban unrest," and the face of that was Black young people. You can't talk about criminalization in this country without understanding the history of Blackness and Black people in this country. Politicians have used us as the fuel to make things happen. We're always the canaries in the coal mine.

For example, let's look at Bill Clinton and the 1994 crime bill. Clinton gives people an ideological basis to continue to do what they've been doing. He was one of the most destructive presidents for Black people, and we're still trying to recover from his reign, including in terms of what he put into place around immigration and immigrant detention; a lot of people don't think about that as Black, but the people who were most incarcerated within immigrant detention are disproportionately Black immigrants.

Scahill: *And, of course, you had this massive atrocity that happened at Guantanamo with Haitians who were fleeing violence that the United States sponsored in the form of overthrowing Jean-Bertrand Aristide. And then you had, and I think a lot of people, particularly young people, don't know this history, before Guantanamo was the place where Bush stuck people extrajudicially in the so-called war on terror, Clinton piled up the bodies inside of Guantanamo of the first independent Black republic in the Western hemisphere, right?*

Kaba: That's right. It came back to haunt Hillary Clinton in Miami with Haitians not voting for her, so people have long memories. But Clinton's welfare reform, or what we call welfare deform, had such an impact, particularly on single Black mothers. The carceral state was reinforced and made much more brutal through the three-strikes laws, through the mandatory minimum sentences which were upped, through his horrific behavior around rushing back to Arkansas during his election to go and put somebody who was mentally disabled to death. He really set in place the apparatus that we are still trying to dismantle today.

Scahill: *Under Obama, you had several incendiary killings that happened. You had George Zimmerman murdering Trayvon Martin. You had the shooting of Mike Brown, and we can go down a whole list of people. I remember as a kid growing up in Milwaukee, the police shooting an unarmed Black man named Ernest Lacy ... What was it about this string of incidents that seemed to rejuvenate a rebellious atmosphere in this country that was in large part led by young African Americans and other people of color across this country? And they weren't being organized by Al Sharpton or some national network; it was a spontaneous response. Given that this has happened from the beginning of this republic to Black people from white people in authority or people with a badge, what was it about that particular moment that seemed to spark this uprising?*

Kaba: Almost every urban uprising in the country's history has police violence at its root. If you look at the 1935 Harlem "riots," or Harlem uprising, at the core of it is a rumor that a young Puerto Rican boy is killed, but he wasn't actually killed, and that sparks the conflagration. In 1943, that rebellion in Harlem, also at the root was Marjorie Polite, and this young man and the police basically being accused of having shot him; that's a conflagration. 1964 is also a young Black man who is shot by the cops in New York City.

If you look at the history of all the different uprisings, going back to the early 1900s, all are sparked by police brutality. The reason that's the case, and has always been the case in this country, is because it is the most clear example of being treated unjustly in the country. It's the clearest way that almost every Black person can see that they are second class. In other things it's diffused. We know there are poor people, but if you yourself are not poor in this country you can pretend they don't exist. And that includes Black people. You can live in a way that ignores Black poor people, except that many, many Black people are tied to poor people anyway. Even if they left their communities, a lot of their families still are struggling, so we see it in a different way. But just not having the right to exist, to walk down the street without being harmed, that consistent knowledge of that is something that . . .

Scahill: *By the people who taxpayers are financing to supposedly keep order and safety.*

Kaba: Exactly, the gatekeepers of the state are turning, literally, their guns on us. And so it is a sight that makes sense where people feel a direct, visceral sense that, "This is frigging unfair. What are they doing to us?" And that's been along the way. I think that's why it's important to put the Movement for Black Lives that continues to happen right now in its proper context. It's only part of a long freedom struggle that has gone on in this country for as long as Black people have been here.

Arresting the Carceral State

with Erica R. Meiners

Jacobin, February 2014

In 2013, the American Civil Liberties Union (ACLU) published a listicle on *Buzzfeed* highlighting the egregious ways young people have been criminalized in American schools.

Titled "Eleven Students Whose Punishments We Wish Were Made Up," examples included "a twelve-year-old student in Texas who was charged with a misdemeanor for spraying herself with perfume and 'disrupting class.'" In another case, a dropped piece of cake in the lunchroom triggered the arrest of a sixteen-year-old California student who, courtesy of a school police officer, ended up with a broken wrist.

Across the nation, eerily similar stories proliferate. Students, particularly those of color, are being pushed out of school and into the criminal legal system through excessive suspensions, expulsions, arrests, and an overreliance on high-stakes testing. Or they are slotted into special education classes—a one-way ticket to an individualized education plan.

Increasing numbers of policy makers, advocates, academics, educators, parents, students, and organizers are focusing explicitly on the relationships between education and imprisonment, also known as the school-to-prison pipeline (STPP). Less a pipeline than a nexus or a swamp, the STPP is generally used to refer to interlocking sets of structural and individual relationships in which youth, primarily of color, are funneled from schools and neighborhoods into under- or unemployment and prisons.

While the US public education system has historically diverted nonwhite communities toward undereducation, non-living-wage work, participation in a permanent war economy, and/or incarceration, the development of the world's largest prison nation over the last three decades has strengthened policy, practice, and ideological linkages between schools and prisons. Nonwhite, nonheterosexual, and gender nonconforming students are targeted for surveillance, suspended and expelled at higher rates, and are much more likely to be charged, convicted, and removed from their homes or otherwise to receive longer sentences.

Criminalizing student behavior is not new. The concept of the "school resource officer" emerged in the 1950s in Flint, Michigan, as part of a strategy to embed police officers in community contexts. In 1975, only 1 percent of US schools reported having police officers. As of 2009, New York City schools employed over five thousand school safety agents and 191 armed police officers, effectively making the school district the fifth largest police district in the country.

This culture of control and surveillance mirrors the intensification of state punishment. Starting in the 1970s—despite a decline in the rates of crime (not always a measure of harm)—states implemented "tough-on-crime" policies that built the world's largest prison population and did not make communities stronger or safer. A carceral logic, or a punishment mind-set, crept into nearly every government function, including those seemingly removed from prisons. Those seeking food stamps are subject to mandatory and/or random drug testing. Immigration and Customs Enforcement has become the largest enforcement agency in the United States. Post–secondary education applications ask about criminal records, and many states bar those with felony convictions from voting.

In K–12 education, high-stakes testing is a proxy for "accountability," and low-performing schools are punished with closure while charter schools continue to open. After a few high-profile school shootings in the early 1990s, states introduced "zero tolerance" discipline policies to address a wide range of behaviors schools identified as undesirable. The subsequent increase in surveillance cameras, security guards, metal detectors, and punitive school discipline policies doubled the number of students suspended from school from 1.7 million a year in 1974 to 3.7 million in 2010. The impact of suspensions is clear. Suspended students are three times more likely to drop out by the tenth grade than peers who have never been suspended.

Paralleling our unjust criminal legal system, students of color are, unsurprisingly, targets in schools. One of every four African American public school students in Illinois was suspended at least once for disciplinary reasons during the 2009–10 school year, the highest rate among the forty-seven states examined by the Center for Civil Rights Remedies.

While overall youth school-based arrests in Chicago Public Schools (CPS) are down from a peak of more than eight thousand in 2003, Black youth are still disproportionately arrested. In 2012, Black students, who represent about 42 percent of the total CPS population, accounted for 75.5 percent of school-based arrests. Again, mimicking what is happening in the juvenile justice system, the vast majority of these school-based arrests are for misdemeanor offenses (84 percent) as opposed to felonies (16 percent).

In other words, youth are not being arrested for serious violent acts or for bringing a weapon to school but for disrespect or "fighting." Often the term used to describe the differentials between white and Black suspension and arrest is "disproportionality," but this term masks the central roles white supremacy and anti-Black racism play in shaping ideas and practices surrounding school discipline.

Yet we won't solve the STPP problem by simply changing school disciplinary policies. Because many states spend more on prisons than education, we have to change funding priorities as well. Take Illinois, for example. Between 1985 and 2005, the state built more than twenty-five new prisons or detention facilities. Over the same span, no new public colleges or universities were established. Funding reform initiatives for K–12 education, mandated by the Illinois Supreme Court, have stalled for decades—ensuring that poor communities and communities of color still receive significantly less money.

The increased reliance on high-stakes testing also contributes to the STPP by encouraging a drill-and-test culture within schools that tends to supplant art, music, and physical education. Many students, finding the curriculum increasingly irrelevant, disengage and are subsequently pushed out of school. In a landscape where market-based reforms have naturalized competition between students and across districts, where failure always results in sanctions, some struggling schools actively weed out students who do not meet the requirements of the test. In Florida, for example, schools have suspended low-performing students in order to improve their overall test results. Encouragingly, students, teachers, and parents have protested this practice of teaching to the test, with calls to treat them as "more than a score."

Additionally, attacks on workplace rights are tied to the carceral logic. Corporate-driven reforms that reshape schools as sites of temporary and unprotected labor constrain school personnel's capacity to interrupt the STPP. We know that students benefit when teachers have workplace protections that foster speech, independent thinking, and advocacy. The push to de-professionalize and de-unionize school personnel—and reframe teachers as Peace Corps lightworkers—transforms teachers into precariously employed charity workers with few rights and meager compensation.

In current circulations of corporate education reform, the image of the lazy, negligent, unionized, female teacher has emerged as a figure to despise. In tandem, the unruly Black and brown children require the discipline and order that can only be achieved through schools' intimate partnership with the police, the military, and the business community. This is a recipe for disaster. As the Chicago Teachers Union repeatedly reminded us in their successful fall 2012 strike, teachers' working conditions are students' learning conditions. If educators are forced to teach to tests that don't actually measure student learning, have no employment security but instead are "at will" workers, and are de-professionalized beyond belief, teachers are significantly less likely to support cultures within schools that resist racial profiling or to build other mechanisms to address harm in their schools.

What to do? We are part of and committed to national and local organizing that is building restorative and transformative justice into schools and communities. These philosophies and practices of justice, in contrast to retributive ones, seek to empower communities to respond holistically to violence and harm. Restorative and transformative justice take into account the needs of those affected by an incident of harm, the contexts that produced or shaped harm, and seek to transform or rebuild what was lost rather than view punishment as a final resolution. We desperately need our schools and communities to become restorative and transformative spaces.

We also know the best way to prevent future incarceration is to invest in people and communities and provide excellent educational opportunities for all. A 2007 study estimated that for each potential dropout who completed high school, the US could save $209,000 in prison and other costs. Why not shift budgets from cops in schools to counselors, from building prisons to opening up additional spaces in free public colleges and universities? Instead of more militarized borders, why not ensure that all youth have access to meaningful, discipline-building co-curricular activities such as music, drama, art, and sports?

These are not just pipe dreams. Communities are pushing back and building the world we need. Groups like Chicago's Community Organizing and Family Issues (COFI) have developed downloadable resources for parents on how to advocate for and build restorative justice practices at their children's schools. (As COFI has documented, implementing community peace rooms staffed by parents and volunteers has reduced suspensions and had a positive effect on attendance and behavior.) In the last few years, a network of community groups has emerged offering both spaces to dialogue and concrete ideas on how everyday people can build safety that is not reliant on criminalization—from New York's Audre Lorde Project, to Chicago's Project NIA, to Oakland's StoryTelling and Organizing Project.

In addition, teachers are changing classroom practices and school cultures by constructing alternatives. Restorative justice is essentially an unfunded initiative, but teachers across the country are hungry for options. In Chicago over the last couple of years, teachers have crowded workshops at the Teachers for Social Justice Curriculum Fair and other sites to learn how to support this paradigm shift and how to build alternatives to harsh disciplinary policies. We participate in, and are excited by, organizing that takes as a starting point the interconnections between struggles to dismantle our carceral state and to build just and flourishing public K–12 educational systems.

These include LGBTQ liberation movements that reject criminalization as the response to gender and sexual violence in schools, immigration rights organizers who say no to legislation that pits children against parents, and anti-violence movements that do not rely on policing as their primary strategy for peace-building. As the Black feminist lesbian poet and scholar Audre Lorde wrote years ago, "There are not single-issue struggles because we do not live single-issue lives."

Arresting the flow of young people from communities into prisons requires rethinking and rebuilding across multiple systems and structures. Schools are just one site for this labor, and we are heartened to see the promising efforts across the country to build them into restorative and transformative spaces.

Itemizing Atrocity

with Tamara K. Nopper
Jacobin, August 2014

According to the *Economist*, "America's police have become too militarized." Not to be outdone, *Business Insider* published an article by Paul Szoldra, a former US marine who professed to be aghast at the scenes of camouflage-wearing, military-weapon-toting police officers patrolling the streets of an American city in armored vehicles. Szoldra quotes one of his Twitter followers, another former soldier, who wrote: "We rolled lighter than that in an actual warzone."

Some may be surprised to see such stories run in magazines like the *Economist* and *Business Insider*, but suddenly discussions about America's militarized police forces are semi-mainstream. In the wake of the police killing of African American teenager Michael Brown in Ferguson, Missouri, and the subsequent riots and protests, social media is littered with images of tear gas, tanks, and police in military gear with automatic weapons—all aimed at Black people in the city.

Several publications and writers have rushed to alert us about their stories on the militarization of the police. Commentators have encouraged us to connect the dots between what is happening overseas and what is happening here. Hashtags referring to Ferguson and Gaza share the same caption. We are told by some that the war on terror has come home.

Presumably, connecting these dots and making these comparisons will offer more clarity about the current situation faced by Ferguson's beleaguered Black residents.

But what will we better see and know? And who and what will be (once again) invisible and unheard in the process?

In her book *Scenes of Subjection*, Saidiya Hartman writes:

Rather than try to convey the routinized violence of slavery and its aftermath through invocations of the shocking and the terrible, I have chosen to look elsewhere and consider those scenes in which terror can hardly be discerned. . . . By defamiliarizing the familiar, *I hope to illuminate the terror of the mundane and quotidian rather than exploit the shocking spectacle.*

Hartman's emphasis on "the terror of the mundane and quotidian" is her attempt to address the dilemma of Black people having their suffering (un)seen and (un)heard by non-Blacks—including those who purport to care:

At issue here is the precariousness of empathy . . . how does one give expression to these outrages without exacerbating the indifference to suffering that is the consequence to the benumbing spectacle or contend with the narcissistic identification that obliterates the other or the prurience that too often is the response to such displays? This was the challenge faced by [Frederick] Douglass and other foes of slavery. . .

A century and a half after Douglass fought against slavery, the police *have* become more militarized in terms of weapons, tanks, training, and gear. SWAT teams have been deployed at an accelerated rate and for an increased number of activities. Reports like the one recently published by the ACLU provide some details about these technologies of war amassed by local police departments.

Julilly Kohler-Hausmann, Radley Balko, and others have explained that the militarization of US police can be traced back to the mid-1960s. For example, in 1968 urban police forces were able to buy new equipment and technologies thanks to funding from the newly passed Safe Streets Act.

The social anxiety and fear engendered by the Vietnam War and domestic urban rebellions led by Black people provided license for the police to turn these new products on the marginalized populations of inner-city America.

SWAT teams, battering rams, and no-knock warrants (immortalized by Gil Scott Heron and written about by James Baldwin), all predate contemporary hyper-militarized police forces. Black people have been the overwhelming targets of these instruments of war. In his 1982 song "Batterram," presaging our current uber-militarized police force, Toddy Tee raps:

> he just might (flatten out every house he sees on sight)
> Because he say the rockman is takin' him for a fool

For Black people, the war on terror hasn't "come 'home.'" It's always been here. How then might we consider the emphasis on the militarization of policing as *the* problem as another example of "the precariousness of empathy"?

The problem with casting militarization as *the* problem is that the formulation suggests it is the *excess* against which we must rally. We must accept that the ordinary is fair for an extreme to be the problem. The policing of Black people—carried out through a variety of mechanisms and processes—is purportedly warranted, as long as it doesn't get *too* militarized and excessive.

Attention is drawn to the "spectacular event" rather than to the point of origin or the mundane. Circulated are the spectacles—dead Black bodies lying in the streets or a Black teenager ambushed by several police officers in military gear, automatic weapons drawn.

Along with these dramatic images, numbers and statistics are the main metric for soliciting empathy and galvanizing people into action. It is the size and power of the gun. It is the number of cops at the scene. It is the tank pointed at protesters. It is the forty-one bullets shot at a Black immigrant standing in his doorway; the eight to ten times a Black teenager was shot "like an animal" when walking to see his relatives or the four hours his body lay in the street while family members and neighbors watched and waited helplessly; the at least eleven times a Black woman was punched by a cop straddling her on the side of a highway; the over two minutes a forty-eight-year-old Black woman, half-naked, was kept in the hallway and surrounded by about a dozen cops after being dragged out of her apartment; the number of Black people stopped and frisked.

The mind-numbing images and numbers keep coming. And shock and awe often greet their arrival. Both the pictures and statistics become the stuff of (at times hard-fought) headlines, reports, social commentaries, and "teachable moments." Sadly, their circulation seems to demonstrate, as Frank Wilderson puts it, that "taxonomy can itemize atrocities but cannot bear witness to suffering."

These images and numbers are not trivial or unimportant. Like the Black people killed, injured, humiliated, and haunted, they matter and shouldn't be ignored. The greater the number of shots fired, the greater likelihood of being hit. The amount of time spent physically contained by cops increases the possibility of harm.

Other Black people have to live with the trauma of having seen and heard these images in real time or virally, the numbers accumulating as they fly and tick away and scream and gasp in the air. Yet we know it only takes one shot from a cop to kill. And as the police killing of Eric Garner shows, it can take no shot at all.

The problem is not just the excess. Yet one gets the sense that the only way to generate a modicum of concern or empathy for Black people is to raise the stakes and to emphasize the extraordinary nature of the violations and the suffering. To circulate repeatedly the spectacular in hopes that people consider the everyday. It's a fool's errand because it often doesn't garner the response desired or needed. And it leaves Black people in the position of having to ratchet up the excess to get anyone to care or pay attention.

What next, some might ask? What more could happen after Ferguson and the hyper-militarization of the police? A bomb dropped on Black people in the United States? That has already been done, decades ago. To the point: spectacle as the route to empathy means the atrocities itemized need to happen more often or get worse, to become more atrocious each round in hopes of being registered.

How does Black suffering register when we are told that it is the militarization of the police that is the problem? Again, Hartman is instructive, writing of "the narcissistic identification that obliterates the other." It is true that militarization is a global phenomenon. It is true that the United States and its allied countries enforce their brutal agendas throughout the world through military force, sanctions, and the war on terror.

It is also true that, despite the Black diaspora's effort to emphasize what happens to Black people worldwide (including in the United States), references to globalization, militarization, and the war on terror are often treated as markers of non-Blackness—and among some progressives, as code for "needing to go beyond Black and white" or for Blacks in the United States to not be so "US-centric" (read: "self-absorbed").

Hence the odd historiography about the militarization of the US police as emerging from the (relatively new) war on terror found in some of the current commentary. Some may promote the effort to "connect the dots" in service of a more nuanced analysis or to encourage international and interracial solidarity.

We can also consider this an example of "the precariousness of empathy," with Black people required to tether their suffering to non-Black people (and processes often erroneously treated as non-Black, such as "militarization" and "globalization") in the hope of being seen and heard. This is also a marker of the compulsory solidarity that is demanded of Black people without any expectation that this solidarity will be reciprocated.

Relatedly, the push for coalition and the use of analogies suggests a difficulty to name precisely what Black people experience in the United States. Scenes of police violence against Black people in Ferguson seemingly become more legible, more readable and coherent, when put into conversation with Iraq or Gaza. Yet something gets lost in translation.

The sentiments—"I thought I was looking at pictures of Iraq but I was looking at America!" or "Ferguson=Gaza" or "now [Black people in the United States] know how the Third World feels"—circulate on social media. Such statements express a belief in American exceptionalism and a certain amount of glee and resentment toward African Americans while professing empathy.

Amid this, we are left with the difficulty to name both the spectacle and the quotidian violence Black people in the United States experience day after day from the police and the racially deputized. What do we call this incessant violence? How do we describe it beyond the spectacular event? Occupation? War? Genocide? Life? Death?

We conclude with more questions: How do we rightfully account for the increased militarization of the police as a problem without forgetting what Joy James reminds us: "The *dreams* and *desires* of a society and state will be centered on the control of the black body"—or as Jared Sexton emphasizes: Black people serve as "the prototypical targets of the panoply of police practices and the juridical infrastructure built up around them."

How do we contend with Wilderson's assertion that "white people are not simply 'protected' by the police. They are—in their very corporeality the police?" What does all this mean when we think about hyper-militarized police forces that weaponize white supremacy against Black bodies and the specter of Blackness among others? How does it feel to be the prototypical target?

What do the spectacles of policing—as well as the responses to it—both reveal and camouflage in regard to the "terror of the mundane and quotidian," a terror that is often taken for granted, even in critical commentary?

"I Live in a Place Where Everybody Watches You Everywhere You Go"

Remarks at the Scholar and Feminist Conference, "Subverting Surveillance: Strategies to End State Violence," Barnard College, New York, February 2018

I live in a place where everybody watches you everywhere you go. As a young Black male, everybody watches you. Police pull you over for no reason. They see you, pull up, tell you, "Put your hands on the car." Most of them just be so disrespectful. They'll tell you, "You ain't nothing, you ain't going to be nothing," or "You're just a waste of time." And most people take that into their head, and they grow up disrespecting, killing, and fighting the police. Also, people watch you when you go into stores. And every hour you see the same employee. You can't shop in peace nowhere. They follow you everywhere. And lastly, the gang members. There is no safe place for you to walk in Chicago. Everywhere you go people ask you the same question: "What you is?" They ask you over and over again. But on most streets, they don't even ask. They shoot first. I've been running from bullets and asked that question since I was twelve. And I don't even gangbang. You can't even listen to some music in most neighborhoods. Some of the rappers get killed because of the stuff they say in their lyrics. You get robbed just coming up the street because people don't know you where you from. Why so many shootings happen in Chicago? Where I'm from people call this place Chiraq.

There are lots of things in what Marquise Paino has to say that are worth excavating and talking about. But I'm going to focus on what he tells us about young Black and brown people in Chicago being constantly watched, by the gatekeepers of the state in the police, by businesses that surveil and follow, making sure that you don't feel like you belong

in those places, and by community members. A question that I would
have liked to have asked Marquise was whether it feels different to be
watched by the cops, the store owners, and the gangs. Is there more or
less fear or anger depending on who is doing the watching?

For Marquise, surveillance really is the norm. It's not an aberra-
tion. And he illustrated that surveillance is never neutral and that it is
situationally weaponized. Marquise demands that we pay attention to
everyday mundane surveillance, the type that is so normalized and so
low-tech as to be considered normal. And warranted so long as it is not
"excessive."

That excess depends a great deal on who the target of the surveillance is. Marquise is inherently presumed guilty. I've worked with a lot
of young people who are in that category, and this category is really the
peculiar vulnerability of Black people in this country. The police and
the business owners and the gang members that Marquise references
see criminality as inscribed in his body, in his being. Either he is in the
process of committing a crime or he has the intention to commit crime
or he is escaping from having committed a crime, or he can be recruited
to crime. Regardless, he is assumed criminal.

That's what I hear from the young folks that I work with all the
time. The idea that young Black people in particular are on some sort of
inevitable march down the path of criminality gives license to surveil,
to watch, to strike them down before they grow. This is a new doctrine
of preemption that's playing out on Black people. A few years ago, a par-
ticipant in Circles and Cyphers—a Chicago-based hip-hop leadership
development program for young people in conflict with the law that my
organization helped to catalyze and incubate for several years—wrote
about his experience with the police in his community:

> Once my friend and I were walking down the street. We were at
> Wood Street and 45th and we had just come outside. Then the cops
> came. Deep. Three cop cars. Because my phone had a weed plant on
> the screen they wanted my PIN number to unlock my phone. But I
> said, "I'm not going to give you my PIN." So one of the white cops
> punched me in my stomach and put me inside the cop car. He told
> me, "You're going to give me that PIN number," and I said, "No."
> Then they let my friend go to his house and took me to my house and

told my mom to unlock my phone. My mom said she didn't know the code. So the white cop left me with my mom and gave my mom the phone. He left.

I went back to the block and saw my friend I had been with earlier and some other guys and told them what happened. I was so mad. And my other friend told me to relax. This is the norm. This is how it is. Get used to it. He and I jumped into the car to pick up his baby girl at school, and I was telling him the details of what happened. I just kept going over it, over and over again. Then the same white cop that took me to my mom's house stopped us and told me to step out of the car. He put me in his cop car and drove me into the territory of another rival gang called La Raza. He dropped me off there. On my way trying to get home I got jumped and almost killed for being in La Raza territory. I ran as fast as I could back to my house.

I called my friend that I had been in the car with and asked him, "What did the cops do to you?" He said they had let him go. Then I had to get off the phone because my baby brother needed my help, so I needed to help him with his homework. Later, when I was finished helping my brother with his homework, my friends came to my house and we smoked some weed.

If you know or work with young people of color, especially young Black people in Chicago and other urban centers, the story that I shared will be really familiar to you. And for years we would complain about the fact that the cops were taking young people we worked with and throwing them in rival gang territory hoping that they would get killed over there. We kept repeating this over and over again, and we would tell people and reporters, and we would make complaints and we would tell politicians and alderpeople.

No one believed the young people or believed us until the Department of Justice report came out a couple of years ago in Chicago and showed that this very thing was the norm and happened a lot. Young people of color feel under siege in their neighborhoods, consistently hassled, harassed, targeted, surveilled, and racially profiled.

In the story of the young person that I quoted—I'm going to call him Willy—the cops are the agents of violence. The cops are actively trying to hurt him. Old-fashioned, non-high-tech tools of surveillance are already destructive and devastating. Perhaps this is my plea that we train ourselves to see the mundane rather than to focus on the spectacular and on the excesses. Young people of color, young Black people in particular, have no presumption of privacy. That idea is an abstraction. So they are disproportionately subjected to bodily searches and seizures through practices like stop and-frisk. Stop-and-frisk for many is just a giant, neon "no-trespassing" sign, for young Black people in urban centers in particular. Their phones, their computers, their bodies are subject to being searched on the streets, in their homes, without cause, at any time. The examples that I've cited suggest that for most young Black and brown people surveillance and being perceived as a threat are just a daily fact of life, not an academic or an analytic exercise.

The vast majority of the country accepts these law-and-order practices as the price of "freedom" and safety. Mass criminalization is also mass surveillance—these things are not separate even if they are treated by some civil libertarians as such. Both are really overwhelmingly confined to communities of color and LGBTQ folks and others who are on the margins. Yet even in those communities many have become inured to the routine violation of rights and liberties. We're told by politicians and law enforcement that these practices are necessary and that they are in fact color-blind. We mostly swallow their propaganda. It doesn't matter that incarceration and oppressive policing and surveillance are actually decimating Black and brown communities across the country and poor white communities as well. Black and brown people know that the state and its gatekeepers exert their control over all aspects of our lives. This is not new.

I'd be interested to know how privacy advocates and some civil libertarians might discuss the concept of surveillance with young people like Marquise and Willy. What's the meaning of data collection by the NSA to a young person who lives under constant scrutiny already? Would Marquise be surprised or disturbed that the cops are looking for new ways to more easily access cell phone information when his cell phone is already being demanded without cause and his mother is being told to give up his password? What does predictive policing or a gang database mean for young people who are being dropped off into rival gang territory so that they can be killed there? What does facial recognition technology mean to young people who are regularly rec-

ognized and hassled by the beat cop in their neighborhood? They don't
need technology for that. They just need their eyes.

I don't know the answer to these questions. But it really seems important for us to understand and to know what that actually means if
we're going to create whatever we're going to create to get out of this
mess that we're in. Finally, an abolition politic interrogates the root
causes of violence that are masked by the carceral state. My friend
scholar and activist Erica Meiners says that liberation under oppression is unthinkable by design. So an abolition politic insists that we
imagine and organize beyond the constraints of the normal. Beyond
mass criminalization, which is an entire system of harassment, violence,
and surveillance that keeps really oppressive gender, class, and racial
hierarchies in place. Our charge is to make imagining liberation under
oppression completely thinkable, to really push ourselves to think beyond the normal in order for us to be able to address the root causes of
people's suffering. That's the politics that we should be focused on, a
politics that attends to the grievances that people have in their day-to-
day life. The everyday. The mundane. Not the spectacular or the excess.

Toward the Horizon of Abolition

Interview by John Duda

Next System Project, November 2017

John Duda: *I wanted to start by asking you about what it means to work for prison abolition with Trump in the White House. What are your thoughts about what's changed and what will stay the same for the kind of organizing to abolish prisons and police you are engaged in?*

Mariame Kaba: I think that one thing that remains constant for me is that the system—the prison-industrial complex—isn't broken. The system of mass criminalization we have isn't the result of failure. Thinking in this way allows me to look at what's going on right now in a clear-eyed way. I understand that white supremacy is maintained and reproduced through the criminal punishment apparatus. That hasn't changed with Trump coming to power, with Jeff Sessions recycling law-and-order rhetoric and some policies. The Feds can set a tone, but most of the substantive criminal punishment policy happens at the state and county level. That means that we have some potential openings. We're seeing this currently in the reinvigorated struggle to end cash bail and pretrial detention, for example.

Frankly, I really didn't think that Donald Trump would win. I was sure that white people would vote for him, but I thought that the votes of people of color would offset this so that he wouldn't actually be president. But I'm not surprised that white people voted for him across the board. I expected that.

This election also destabilized some ideas I had about politics and electoral organizing, because I did believe that mobilization would lose to organization. We'd been led to believe by the Democratic Party that they had all these offices on the ground, all these volunteers, that they had the data analytics to identify who their voters were, and that they could turn them out. I understood, through my study and participation at some points in my life in electoral organizing, that organization trumps mobilization—and I thought the Dems had that down, frankly, and they did not, clearly.

I'm still trying to figure out what all of this means for anti-criminalization organizing. Some people are lamenting the fact that the DOJ is going to revert back to what it was before the Obama administration. I have actually been very upset over the past few years about the impulse people have to rely on law enforcement to police the police—also people saying they want to prosecute "killer cops," demanding that the DOJ step in. I've always felt that was futile. The cops won't police themselves, and I've thought that the strategy of turning to the DOJ for relief acted like a cooling saucer, as it demobilizes action. Every time someone is murdered by police: "Let the DOJ handle it, let the DOJ handle it!" It's not an effective strategy and it sucks up so much activist energy.

Now that people can't say "let the DOJ handle it," I wonder about openings for people to consider other things.

Duda: *That kind of shrunken imagination seems to really hold back a lot of people from thinking about a world without prisons. Do you have a sense of why? What's the source of this blockage?*

Kaba: I heard Patrisse Cullors from the Black Lives Matter Global Network say that somebody had to actually first imagine prisons and the police themselves in order to create them. Everything you see in the world—somebody thought of it first. I think that's right. Once things are actualized into the world and exist, you can't imagine how the world functioned before it. It's like we develop amnesia. You just assume things have always been as they are. I see this in myself . . .

The other thing about prisons and police is how they make people—the vast majority of people—feel secure. *I don't mean safe, I mean secure.* Secure means that the scary, awful, monster people are kept at bay by those institutions. That is the story that gets told and reinforced by media, by our parents, by our culture. That is our story.

My comrade Paula Rojas has written that the cops are in our heads and hearts. Therefore, this system is naturalized in a way that makes it almost impossible for folks to step back and think that it wasn't always like this.

But, again, we can't underestimate the fact that we think these institutions keep us secure. Security and safety aren't the same thing. Security is a function of the weaponized state that is using guns, weapons, fear, and other things to "make us secure," right? Horrible things are supposed to be kept at bay by these tools, even though we know that horrible things continue to happen all the time—and that these very tools and the corresponding institutions are reproducing the violence and horror they are supposed to contain.

All of these things are pretty clear to a whole bunch of people—we just, I think, don't want to have to think hard about what else might be possible.

Duda: *I think that kind of long-term clarity about what it is that this work is ultimately about is really important. I think about the history here: scholars like Naomi Murakawa and Elizabeth Hinton have built off of the work of Angela Davis, tracing out the history of how people who thought they were making the prisons more fair or making sentencing less biased, really just super-charged the apparatus of mass incarceration. As more and more people become aware that there is a problem with prisons, are you worried about a similar kind of effect in the long term?*

Kaba: Absolutely. It contributes to my insomnia. It is my constant preoccupation. Davis helps us to understand that the PIC itself is a product of various reforms over time, that even the prison itself was a reform. I reiterate to people all the time: *We cannot reform police. We cannot reform prisons.* We cannot.

Telling people this can foster a sense of despair; it can demobilize people in real ways. It can make people feel like everything is inevitably going to remain this way: this is where we're at, this is where things are going to be.

But when you say things can't be reformed, the question becomes how do you handle people who are in immediate need for relief, right? How are you going to make life livable for people living in unlivable circumstances?

People think that either you're interested in reform or you're an abolitionist—that you have to choose to be in one camp or the other. I don't think that way. For some people, reform is the main focus and end goal and for some people, abolition is the horizon. But I don't know anybody who is an abolitionist who doesn't support *some* reforms.

Mainly those reforms are, to use the term coined by André Gorz and popularized by Ruth Wilson Gilmore here in the United States, *non-reformist reforms*. Which reforms don't make it harder for us to dismantle the systems we are trying to abolish? Don't make it harder to create new things? What "non-reformist" reforms will help us move toward the horizon of abolition? Sometimes people who you love dearly want you to fight for their reformist reform. They want you to fight for something they think will benefit a small tiny sliver of the people harmed by this behemoth monster without consideration for how it would then entrench other things that would make life harder for other people.

That's the case when you think about the conversation around nonviolent, non-sexual-offending prisoners. We focus a bunch of attention on getting those people out. But in doing so we make it impossible for people who have used violence—the majority of the state prison population, by the way—to ever get out.

There's this fight that the way to abolish the death penalty is to commute everybody to life without parole. And I just can't get behind that. That's still physical, social, and civic death. "But at least they're alive . . . " That to me is an absolute perfect example of a reformist reform, which actually makes it less likely that we're going to get people out of jail and prisons.

Some reforms end up reproducing the system in another form. I was listening to Robin D. G. Kelley, and he mentioned that you put out some kind of a reform, and then that reform becomes institutionalized. Worse than institutionalization, the reform actually creates a new form of consciousness and a new form of "common sense." That reform itself becomes the new common sense, and that's so dangerous on so many levels.

Duda: *I really like the blog post you did in 2014 that was composed of a list of very simple, very straightforward questions about this question—it's like a test you can use to tell if something is a reform you should support, with* *questions like "Does it rely on technology?" or "Does it give the police more money?" Are there any other "reformist reforms" that you'd add to your original list if you were updating it?*

Kaba: Well, the first thing I'll say is how that post came about. I wrote it so quickly! I was asked some questions by several young organizers who identify as abolitionists and who were struggling mightily when all these proposals around body cameras were coming out. These organizers wanted to support *something*, but didn't know what and didn't think they knew how to figure that out on their own. I wrote that piece very fast, and put it out on my blog. It went viral—somebody emailed me from London to say that they're using it there. I was like, "My God, that's really amazing and great for something to be helpful to a lot of people. . . . "

Rachel Herzing (a cofounder of Critical Resistance) and I ended up writing a very short piece about our concerns around community oversight boards and community control of police, for some young folks who had asked us questions in Chicago when the whole oversight board stuff happened with Mayor Rahm Emanuel. They wanted suggestions about what language to use, how to think about this, how to respond.

We wrote something up and shared it with a bunch of abolitionists, and we got a range of responses. On the one hand, we had people saying this is ridiculous, these bodies are just going to reproduce what we currently have and what we currently have has no power to oversee the police. By the very nature of policing, it's just not possible.

But then there were people who thought that maybe what we need to do is to mobilize the community outside of those structures so they don't get fooled into thinking these structures are actually going to be able to do anything. And some people thought that if you had a body that had the ability to hire and fire and to control resources, then it's possible that this could be an interim way to begin to erode the power of the police. In that case it would be part of the long evolution on your way to abolition. You're taking away power from the institution of policing.

I'm conflicted. I go back and forth all the time. Is this possible? Aren't the police and policing itself is too strong to allow any civilian body to control it? Don't they have unions so powerful that they almost always cow civilian leadership? How then would this oversight body survive that?

I'm thinking about that right now because there's a historical demand from Black communities, since the Panthers, if not before, to have community control of the police. My question is, can this be possible? Can the community have power over the institution of policing? Is that possible for us? We don't have power over our military; how do we propose to have power over the police, over the whole surveillance apparatus? I don't know. That's what I continue to think about these days.

Duda: *So, if community control over the police is not going to be a step that necessarily we want to bet everything on, what do we do instead? I know there are a lot of alternatives that are really promising around reconciliation, around restorative justice, around ways of addressing and reducing harm through dialogue, but what about alternatives for the function that the police, theoretically, have—to help people escape situations in which they might be harmed? Obviously, they don't serve this function perfectly, by any stretch of the imagination. But are there alternative practices around that that you can point to that you think are more promising than the police in this regard?*

Kaba: I will say this: I think community accountability and work in our communities is key. We have to get serious about doing that work and reaching toward each other. If our relationships are transformed over time, we'll be able to think more clearly about more ways to reduce harm. At that point—maybe our society won't need armed people to come to our houses to do wellness checks. Maybe the very fact that we have created a different society for ourselves—have established a different way of relating to one another—answers the question for us eventually.

Living the way we live makes it difficult for most people to seriously consider the end of policing. The idea that cops equal security is difficult to dislodge. To transform this mind-set, where cops equal security, means we have to actually transform our relationships to each other enough so that we can see that we can keep each other safe. You cannot have safety without strong, empathic relationships with others. You can have security without relationships but you cannot have safety—actual safety—without healthy relationships. Without getting to really know your neighbor, figuring out when you should be intervening when you hear and see things, feeling safe enough within your community that you feel like, yeah, my neighbor's punching their partner, I'm going to

knock on the door, right? I'm not going to think that that person's going to pull a gun on me and shoot me in the head. I don't believe that
because I know that person. I know them. I built that relationship with
them and even though they're upset and mad I'm taking the chance of
going over there and being like, "You need to stop this now, what are
you doing?" Part of what this necessitates is that we have to work with
members of our communities to make violence unacceptable. What my
friend Andy Smith has said is that this is a problem of political organizing and not one of punishment.

How can we organize to make interpersonal violence unthinkable?
That necessitates transformation on so many levels for many people.
But it doesn't necessitate it, actually, for some other groups, who have
never had the option of calling the police—they just haven't—and
they've been managing to take care of each other and themselves outside of that option.

Our questions answer themselves if we look right in front of our
nose. People ask me all the time what abolition looks like. You know,
there are groups of people who are living a type of abolition now. I want
you to think of affluent, white neighborhoods in the Chicago area like
Naperville where there are no cops to be found . . . anywhere. You actually have to call them to show up. Their kid's schools? No cops, no
metal detectors. They have what they need. The people are working.
Talk about full employment! People have houses that are worth millions. They've got housing, healthcare, jobs: all the things to make it so
people won't feel we need police, prisons, and surveillance. There are
some communities already living that today.

The question is why for them and not for all of us? I think to some
degree imagination is necessary . . . yes. But we don't have to imagine
that far into the future. It's here.

We have to stop making things so complicated and seeming so fan-
tastic around abolition. "Oh my gosh, abolition doesn't make sense!
How would we ever do that?" I'm like: "You're doing it right now." Certain people's race and status protect them, and that protection needs to
be possible for everybody.

Duda: *I was reading about some of the alternative practices that have developed in Chicago. They are amazing and inspiring—but they are also incred-*

ible amounts of hard work. For instance, the mothers who were setting up on a street corner every day with hot dogs, hundreds and hundreds of hot dogs, to reduce violence in their neighborhood.

Kaba: Yep. Exactly. By the way, those mothers were kicked out from in front of a building that was vacant. They can't be on a corner outside an empty building because the landlord doesn't want them there. Eventually they worked it out, but that was a lesson to me. They were just sitting outside, but in space that's owned by somebody. And they have a right to then tell you that you can't be there, even though you live next door.

Duda: *I'm wondering how these practices become the norm. We want people doing this all over the place. But the people who are going to be most affected by these things are going to be the least well-resourced to do these things.*

Kaba: Yes.

Duda: *If you're working three jobs and then you have to go and spend eight hours, ten hours, thirty hours doing this work to keep your community safe and to bring your community together, where is the resource stream that supports this? And is there a danger, if this support comes from the state or a large nonprofit, of this kind of work becoming something that reinforces rather than challenges the PIC?*

Kaba: That's a big part of what I'm trying to make sense of. My organization, Project NIA, was started to develop these alternatives, most of which are undertaken by regular folks, just people on their blocks in their communities. A lot of this stuff is not even documented. There are no books about people handling situations as they come up in their neighborhoods.

Can these kinds of practices be sustained if we don't get funders? When funders fund something you're really at their mercy. You're in the position where you're dependent on the foundation or a small grant or whatever for service delivery. It's never enough money. You are always running to try and sustain that funding. You don't have enough paid staff, it's run by volunteers overwhelmingly. You end up having this level of real burnout that happens amongst so many people who are taking on these projects. That's real.

That's to say that I don't really have an answer to whether or not it makes sense to take foundation money or other money to do this work.

I think people should get paid for their labor. But paid doesn't necessarily mean money. . . . Maybe it's got to be free housing, maybe it's got to be free food from the community farm. Maybe that's what's going to happen to us once we get postcapitalism, I don't know. People's labor needs to be acknowledged, rewarded in some way, because it is time, it is effort, it is energy.

We've taken the position at Project NIA to never take state dollars. We refused government grants. We always relied on foundations and individual donations.

Foundations are not perfect, of course. They're part of maintaining the status quo, therefore the handmaidens of capitalism in their own right. What does it mean for a rich person to extract money that should be going to the country's tax base and then decide for themselves how to donate it to the public again? When it's really our money? When they aren't accountable to the public? All those questions are valid. I was a member of INCITE! Women, Gender Nonconforming, and Trans People of Color Against Violence. The conversation about the prison-industrial complex, the nonprofit industrial complex, the revolution not being funded: all those things come, in part, out of INCITE's work. I get all of that, but at the same time those mothers on the street every day need resources to do the work that they are doing. It's not like they've got people throwing money at them. People aren't. They need money, they need people, they need resources. In the end everybody is going to have to do what they think is ethical for themselves. People have to make decisions for themselves.

What are our politics? How do we think that outside resources are going to shape what we're trying to do? Are we prepared for that? Do we want that? I think that's a big issue in terms of thinking about how these things get sustained over time. I do think the important thing to make people understand is that they are happening. There are a bunch of emerging organizations working on transformative justice–based alternatives—but I also want to be clear to acknowledge there are so many people in need, and that we don't have that much capacity. We don't have the capacity to take on hundreds of people if they come to us right now for alternatives. We just don't have it.

PART V

We Must Practice and Experiment: Abolitionist Organizing and Theory

Police Torture, Reparations, and Lessons in Struggle and Justice from Chicago

Prison Culture, February 2015

The national protests catalyzed by the killing of Mike Brown in Ferguson last August continue even as many (including the mainstream media) have moved on. Some critics have suggested that the uprisings are leaderless, lack concrete demands, or are without clear strategy. Each of these critiques is easily refuted, so I won't concern myself with them here.

In Chicago, many have used the energy and opening created by these ongoing protests to reanimate existing long-term anti–police violence campaigns. Hundreds of people gathered at the Chicago Temple to show our love for police torture survivors on the day after Jon Burge was released from house arrest. The gathering was billed as a people's hearing and rally in support of a reparations ordinance currently stalled in the Chicago City Council. Politicians, faith leaders, and community activists spoke at the event. Poets exhorted the crowd. But the most impactful, poignant, and powerful words came from the Burge torture survivors themselves.

They spoke of the impact(s) of the police torture on their lives: the false confessions, the years of incarceration, the mental and physical trauma, the years away from loved ones, the feelings of anger, and ultimately the triumph of still standing in spite of the brutal violence.

As I listened, I was struck again by the importance of language and of words that need to be spoken. Our best teachers, including Audre Lorde among others, have imparted this truth. In the last few months, weeks, and days, I have found myself saying #BlackLivesMatter out loud at various times. It's not that I don't already know that they do. I think that I am trying to speak the words into existence. These words should be taken for granted. They are not. I've revised my previous belief that the words should remain unspoken. "Who are they trying to convince?" I'd previously confided to a friend. It turns out that I owe a debt of gratitude to Opal, Patrisse, and Alicia for reminding me of the power of language and the spoken word.

We are committed here in Chicago to *making* Black lives matter. The reparations ordinance is one concrete way that some of us have chosen to fight to make them matter. Through this decades-long struggle, we are prefiguring the world that we want to inhabit. Again, we have learned from Lorde:

> At the same time as we organize behind specific and urgent issues, we must also develop and maintain an ongoing vision, and the theory following upon that vision, of why we struggle—of the shape and taste and philosophy of what we wish to see.

It's not that Black lives will matter to others within this country when we win the ordinance. Rather, it's that we who struggle together will have defined (in part) the vision of what we mean by Black lives mattering. Through the ordinance, we reject the torture of Black people. We demand that Black people's torture be included in public school curriculum. We demand a formal apology from the city for the harm. We demand resources to heal, including mental heath care, employment, and free education for survivors and their families. We demand financial compensation for the harm done. The Burge torture survivors' reparations ordinance embodies (in part) what we mean when we say that #BlackLivesMatter. It provides a template for demands that should be met for all Black people living in this country.

Every time that I travel to DC I try to visit the Vietnam War Memorial brilliantly designed by Maya Lin. I never want to forget the folly of the nation and the tragedy of war. Seeing thousands upon thousands of names carved into that wall is profoundly jarring every time. With that imagery in mind, I wanted to create a living public memorial at the end of Saturday's rally. Using flags that were made and previously used by the Chicago Torture Justice Memorials, rally participants braved freezing temperatures to create a wall with their bodies at Daley Plaza.

It was our wall of names, the survivors of a war declared and prosecuted against Black people in a major American city. Everyone stood shoulder to shoulder holding a flag with the name of a Burge torture survivor. The line stretched the length of a block. One hundred eighteen documented names. There are many others unknown to us. We honored those people, too, with our public memorial.

It is hard to look at torture. We want to avert our gaze. We want to keep it abstract and to speak euphemistically. But we must squarely face torture; we must see it. This is the only way that we'll have any chance of addressing the violence done in our names at home and abroad. It is abhorrent. We cannot allow ourselves to be complacent. We mustn't continue to tolerate the intolerable. To do so is to forfeit the right to consider oneself to be a moral being. Burge and his fellow officers tortured people in our backyard. We have a collective responsibility to fight for justice for their victims.

It was fitting that we gathered on Valentine's Day. After all, the struggle for justice for Burge torture survivors is a love story. On Saturday, Chicagoans demonstrated love through their presence and by committing to continued action. bell hooks has written:

> It is essential to our struggle for self-determination that we speak of
> love. For love is the necessary foundation enabling us to survive the
> wars, the hardships, the sickness, and the dying with our spirits in-
> tact. It is love that allows us to survive whole.

I am not sure that it is possible for Black people in this country to "survive whole" even as we center love in our lives and our movements for justice. I do know, however, that love offers the opportunity to build sustaining and affirming communities that can help buffer against the relentless forces of oppression seeking our daily destruction. To lead with love gives us a fighting chance at winning. The people who gathered at the Chicago Temple were there to shape a future where we can all be free. Together, we insisted that the affront to the humanity of the torture survivors is a blow against all of us. There was no better message to deliver on Valentine's Day.

Police Torture, Reparations, and Echoes from the "House of Screams"

Prison Culture, May 2015

Yesterday the Chicago City Council passed historic legislation to provide reparations for Burge police torture survivors. The package that was approved includes:

> A formal apology for the torture; specialized counseling services to the Burge torture survivors and their family members on the South Side; free enrollment and job training in City Colleges for survivors and family members (including grandchildren) as well as prioritized access to other City programs, including help with housing, transportation and senior care; a history lesson about the Burge torture cases taught in Chicago Public Schools to 8th and 10th graders; the construction of a permanent public memorial to the survivors; and it sets aside $5.5 million for a Reparations Fund for Burge Torture Victims that will allow the survivors with us today to receive financial compensation for the torture they endured.

Chicago is the first municipality in the United States to legislate reparations for survivors and victims of racist police violence. This victory was an improbable one. In his book *Unspeakable Acts, Ordinary People* published in 2000, journalist John Conroy offered a bleak assessment of the city's response to allegations about Burge and his henchmen's torture:

> The citizens of Chicago were unmoved. The clergy showed no leadership; with the exception of a few mostly low-ranking ministers, religious officials were silent. In the absence of any clamor, politicians showed no interest. Reporters, hearing no complaint, conducted no investigations, and editorial writers launched no crusades. State and federal prosecutors, feeling no pressure from the press or the public, hearing no moral commentary from the religious quarter, prosecuted no one. Judges, seeing no officer indicted and hearing no officer speak against his comrades, could therefore comfortably dismiss claims of torture, and with few exceptions, they did. I found I did not have to journey far to learn that torture is something we abhor only when it is done to someone we like, preferably someone we like who lives in another country.

Fifteen years later, I listened from the third floor of City Hall as the mayor and members of the City Council apologized for the torture endured by over one hundred and eighteen Black people at the hands of Burge and his henchmen. It was a miraculous moment.

What changed between Conroy's description of an apathetic public response to allegations of Burge's torture and yesterday's council vote on reparations? I actually think that Conroy was too dismissive of the organizing that took place in the 1990s. He thought that the protests were mostly insignificant and small. It's a reminder, I think, that our perspectives on historical moments that we inhabit can sometimes be myopic. Conroy could not have known that the organizing in the '90s would serve as a foundation and a road map for efforts into the future. He was right that the political class, the fourth estate, and most of the public were generally apathetic about the allegations of police torture. But I think that he also underestimated the importance of the sustained resistance led by groups like Citizens Alert, Black People Against Torture, the People's Law Office, and more. There were small victories along the way. Our historic achievement yesterday is owed to those hard-fought wins. The organizing and activism that began in the late '80s took the form of protests, advocacy, litigation, and storytelling (including Conroy's powerful investigative journalism). Struggle and organizing matter. Change is too often slow. But sometimes we do win.

I became immersed in the Burge reparations campaign last fall. Over the past six months, a coalition of individuals and groups organized tirelessly to pass this legislation. We held rallies, sing-ins, marches, light actions, train takeovers, exhibition-ins, and more. The price of being immersed in this struggle is to be a witness to unspeakable acts of cruelty committed against other human beings. Burge and his fellow police officers electrocuted, beat, suffocated, and generally tortured dozens of people over two decades. The rooms where commander Jon Burge and his fellow officers tortured and forced confessions from suspects were called the "House[s] of Screams." Those screams echoed in my head yesterday as I heard the Chicago City Council vote on the reparations legislation for survivors of Burge's torture. Slowly those screams became whispers: "Thank you for believing us and for refusing to forget," they seemed to say.

To focus on such harms is painful and can lead to despair. Yet by organizing for some justice for torture survivors, I've seen and experienced incredible kindness, selflessness, and compassion. This is what sustains my hope. I'm convinced that injustice and oppression will not have the last word. Last night I attended a gathering of friends and comrades who have in their own ways contributed to this struggle. Some have spent the better part of three decades fighting to bring some justice to the torture survivors. I was asked to say a few words, and I had difficulty expressing my feelings and thoughts. As I reached for my words, I was overcome at seeing the now old Black men standing before me. A couple had been brutalized in the early 1970s. I wasn't eloquent last night, but my words were heartfelt. I held it together, but when I got home, I cried. They were tears of relief, gratitude, and most of all of love.

There will be time in the coming days and weeks to reflect and to find my words. But for today, let it be known that here in Chicago, we were determined not to forget the atrocities committed in our names by the police. We resisted the violence of fading memories and fought to preserve the knowledge of atrocities for which we all bear some responsibility. We struggled with survivors of torture, and yesterday we won.

Free Us All:
Participatory Defense Campaigns
as Abolitionist Organizing

The New Inquiry, May 2017

How do we free millions of people currently caged in prisons and jails in the United States? As an abolitionist who believes that we must create the conditions for dismantling prisons, police, and surveillance, I'm often asked how to build new institutions that will ensure actual safety. My answer is always the same: collective organizing. Currently, there are a range of decarceral/anticarceral strategies being employed across the country to free prisoners, individually and collectively. People are organizing for bail reform, taking on individual parole support for prisoners, engaging in court watches, launching mass commutation campaigns, and advocating for laws that will offer new pathways for release.

Another important strategy to secure the freedom of criminalized people is participatory defense campaigns. These are grassroots efforts to pressure authorities, attend to prisoner needs, and raise awareness and funds. This essay argues that defense campaigns for criminalized survivors of violence like Bresha Meadows and Marissa Alexander are an important part of a larger abolitionist project. Some might suggest that it is a mistake to focus on freeing individuals when all prisons need to be dismantled. But this argument renders the people who are currently in prison invisible, and thus disposable, while we are organizing toward an abolitionist future. In fact, organizing popular support for prisoner releases is necessary work for abolition. Opportunities to free people from prison through popular support, without throwing other prisoners under the bus, should be seized.

*Defense Campaigns as a Practice of Abolitionist Care**

An important abolitionist insight is that most prison reforms tend to entrench the prison system and expand its reach. Nineteenth-century reformers, for instance, created women's prisons to ameliorate the brutal conditions faced by women who had to share quarters with men in prison. But the result was that exponentially more women were incarcerated.

Consequently, it is important to develop strategies that actually reduce the number of people being incarcerated. Defense campaigns are one such strategy. They are an important strategy, allowing abolitionists to address the needs of incarcerated people without inadvertently strengthening the prison system.

Of course, defense campaigns are most effective as abolitionist strategies when they are framed in a way that speaks to the need to abolish prisons in general. The campaign cannot be framed by a message such as: "This is the one person who shouldn't be in prison, but everyone else should be." Rather, individual cases should be framed as emblematic of the conditions faced by thousands or millions who should also be free.

Speaking at an event celebrating Christina Sharpe's new book *In the Wake*, Saidiya Hartman remarked that "care is the antidote to violence." Her words offer a potentially powerful feminist frame for abolition. Effective defense campaigns provide thousands of people with opportunities to demonstrate care for criminalized individuals through various tactics (including letter writing, financial support, prison visits, and more).

They connect people in a heartfelt, direct way that teaches specific lessons about the brutality of prisons. And this can change minds and hearts, helping people to (hopefully) develop more radical politics. In the end, a practice of abolitionist care underscores that our fates are intertwined and our liberation is interconnected. As such, defense campaigns guided by an ethic and practice of care can be powerful strategies to lead us toward abolition.

---

* I'm indebted to my friend Alisa Bierria for her help in conceptualizing "abolitionist care" practices and tactics.

The Paradox of "Protection" for Black Girls and Women

I've devoted most of my adult life to supporting and organizing with Black women and girls. Most recently, I've been part of cofounding local defense committees for Marissa Alexander and Bresha Meadows.

Bresha Meadows was fourteen years old last July when she allegedly used the gun that her father had brandished for years against her and her family (terrorizing and abusing them) to shoot him in his sleep. Bresha had learned to fear her father who had repeatedly made threats to kill her and her family. The evidence of her father's abuse could be seen in police reports, orders of protection, faded bruises, stories from neighbors, cries for help to school counselors, and rumors of sexual violence.

On more than one occasion, Bresha escaped. Each time she was returned to her abusive home. The last time, she ran to her aunt's home. Her aunt is a police officer, but she could not protect her niece. Instead, Bresha has been charged with aggravated murder. The state didn't protect her, and now she enters her tenth month in jail. Bresha has repeatedly been placed under suicide watch and is facing trial. The state of Ohio is now her abuser.

In late January 2017, as Bresha was being moved from the Trumbull County Juvenile Detention Center for evaluation at a mental health facility, Marissa Alexander was throwing off the shackles of her ankle monitor after two years of house arrest and three years of incarceration before that.

Marissa's journey through the criminal punishment system began in 2010 when she was confronted by her estranged husband in her home, nine days after giving birth to her third child, a little girl. Menaced by a man who admitted in a deposition to having abused every woman he'd ever been partnered with except one, Marissa used a gun that she was licensed to own and fired a single warning shot into the air to ward off her abusive husband.

For this, a jury of her so-called peers found her guilty of aggravated assault with a deadly weapon in a twelve-minute deliberation. Prosecutors used that deadly weapon charge to recommend that Marissa be sentenced under Florida's mandatory minimum gun law to a twenty-year sentence. A judge who had previously ruled that Marissa was ineligible to invoke Stand Your Ground as a defense because she didn't appear afraid said that his hands were tied by the law and ratified the twenty-year sentence.

Bresha and Marissa, a Black girl and a Black woman, are part of the US legacy of criminalizing survivors of violence for self-defense. This is particularly true for women and gender nonconforming people of color (especially Black people) who are inherently seen as threats, who are never vulnerable, who cannot be afraid, who are always the aggressors, and whose skin is weaponized, making it impossible for them to be considered victims of violence. Women and gender nonconforming people of color seem, under the law and in popular consciousness, to have no selves to defend.

Black women and girls in the United States have long sought protections from the state for interpersonal violence while simultaneously organizing against the violence of state power. Ida B. Wells-Barnett was one of the earliest Black women activist-intellectuals to take up Black women's physical and sexual vulnerability as a public concern. The case that she made against lynching was not simply that white people were lying when they said that they were primarily targeting Black male rapists, but also that sexual violence against Black women and girls was ignored and covered up by those same white people. For Wells, and some of the Black club women of the nineteenth and early twentieth centuries, state protection was considered a right of citizenship.

Black women are (more often than not) targets of state violence, and when or if ever they are protected by the punishing state, the costs are very high indeed. In some cases, the "gendered paternalism" of the state (a term coined by lesbian and radical feminists of the 1970s) uses Black women as pawns to reinforce racialized criminalization. For "their own protection" and often against their stated wishes, victims of domestic violence are threatened with jailing by some prosecutors or judges if they refuse to testify against their abusers. Over the years, however, the contradictions of demanding protection from the state that also targets and kills us have proved irreconcilable.

It's easy to understand why the oppressed and marginalized want the criminal punishment system to apply its laws equally. Everyone wants accountability when they experience harm. Endless years of activist energy have been expended in reaction to and reinforcement of this corrupt criminal punishment system. But we have to contend with the fact that the system will never indict itself and that when we demand more prosecutions and punishment this only serves to reinforce a system that must itself be dismantled. As Baldwin teaches us: "The law is meant to be my servant and not my master, still less my torturer and my murderer. To respect the law, in the context in which the American Negro finds himself, is simply to surrender his self-respect."

#FreeBresha and #FreeMarissa in Historical Context

Marissa and Bresha's freedom campaigns were inspired by the 1974 effort to free Joan Little, a twenty-year-old Black woman prisoner. Defending herself against Clarence Allgood, a white guard who was sexually assaulting her, Joan Little grabbed an ice pick from his hand and stabbed him. Allgood died and Little escaped, eventually turning herself in to authorities a week later and claiming self-defense. She was charged with first-degree murder, which carried a possibility of the death penalty. Her plight soon inspired a mass defense campaign that became known as the Free Joan Little Movement. Organizations and individuals across the country raised money for her bond and her defense.

When Little's trial began on July 15, 1975, five hundred supporters rallied outside the Wake County Courthouse. According to historian Danielle McGuire's *At the Dark End of the Street: Black Women, Rape, and Resistance*, the supporters "hoisted placards demanding the court 'Free Joan Little' and 'Defend Black Womanhood,' and loud chants could be heard over the din of traffic and conversation. 'One, two, three. Joan must be set free!' the crowd sang. 'Four, five, six. Power to the ice pick!'"

Eventually, after a five-week trial and seventy-eight minutes of deliberation, Joan Little was acquitted by a jury and returned to prison to serve time for her original offense, which was a break-in. The case is recognized as the first time a woman was acquitted of murder on the grounds of self-defense against rape. It continues to stand as a testament to Black women's resistance to subjugation and sexual predation.

The Free Joan Little Movement is the only example of mass mobilization against state violence on behalf of Black women in the US to date. The Joan Little defense committee organizers focused their campaign on state violence rather than state protection from violence.

They remixed the politics of safety and violence and centered the experiences of women of color in their organizing. They underscored the ways in which the state compounded rather than alleviated violence in the lives of marginalized women.*

This was unprecedented in its time and remains rare today. The work of the Free Joan Little Movement approximates what some "justice" looks like: Joan Little alive, with as much love, solidarity, and community support for her as she would perhaps have had in the glare of death.

The #FreeBresha and #FreeMarissa campaigns, like the Free Joan Little defense campaign that came before it, have taken great pains to underscore that each survivor is one among thousands of Black women and girls who have been and who continue to be criminalized for taking actions to survive. The message now, as it was then, is that all of the Joans, Marissas, and Breshas should be free.

Today's organizers work in the lineage of these lesbian and radical feminists whose politics found their expression in collective defense (a term coined by historian Emily Hobson) and who adopted an organizing strategy of opposition to US state violence. These were feminists who used the politics of collective, mass defense to challenge the intersections of gendered violence and racialized criminalization. These are feminists who would say, in the words of former political prisoner Susan Saxe, "My feminism does not drive me into the arms of the state, but even further from it."

Abolitionist Organizing in Practice

For many survivors, especially of color, the experiences of domestic violence and rape are inextricably linked with systems of incarceration, policing, and criminalization. As many as 94 percent of the population in some women's prisons have a history of having been abused before being caged. Once incarcerated, many cis women, trans women, and gender nonconforming people experience sexual violence from guards and others.†

While this essay focuses particularly on the plight of criminalized

---

* See historian Emily Thuma's work for more detailed information about the Free Joan Little Movement.

† The work of the #FreeBresha and #FreeMarissa campaigns is centered around these experiences as they've organized for the freedom of all criminalized survivors.

survivors of violence, they are just one example where participatory defense campaigns resonate due to revictimization by the state and denial of self-defense. From an abolitionist perspective, all prisoners should be freed. There is a long history of participatory defense campaigns that have focused on people criminalized for dissent or for actions taken as part of social justice organizing (see cases of the Black Panther Party, American Indian Movement, and MOVE members, among others). Abolitionist organizing eschews the idea of "innocence" as salient in dismantling the prison-industrial complex.

I am a co-organizer of Survived & Punished, a coalition of individuals and organizations committed to eradicating the criminalization of survivors of domestic and sexual violence. The members of S&P believe that creating participatory defense campaigns to support the people made most vulnerable to criminalization is essential for educating the public, including prison reformers and abolitionists, about the racial and gendered terror of criminalization and incarceration. We know that campaigns that uplift and defend Black women charged with violent acts, like Marissa and Bresha, are often the only means for securing their freedom.

They are also necessary for popular education to strengthen our movements: both by informing and improving overall movement strategies, and by challenging false and damaging binaries that we use to describe incarcerated people, like violent/nonviolent and innocent/guilty. Defense campaigns can create new forms of learning and practice necessary for abolition. By putting in conversation campaigns like those supporting people in immigrant detention, those criminalized for sex work, and people targeted by transphobic violence, we can better understand how anti-Black gendered violence and criminalization operate.

However, these short-term strategies need to be placed within a longer-term vision for justice rather than as a substitute for that vision. Thus, it is important first to be clear about the limitations and dangers of some of these strategies. Second, we need to look at how we could reframe this struggle to address the systemic nature of white supremacy, settler colonialism, and anti-Blackness. Then it may be easier to coordinate a short-term strategy to support rather than contradict our longer-term vision.

Participatory defense campaigns can be a short-term strategy to act in solidarity with criminalized survivors of violence and all incarcerated people.

If you are now convinced to take up the invitation to create abolitionist defense campaigns in support of criminalized survivors of violence and all incarcerated people, here are some key ideas to keep in mind to guide your organizing:

• Women and gender nonconforming people are not only targets of interpersonal violence but also of state violence. Therefore, discussions of interpersonal violence without a critique of state power and capitalism are at best incomplete and at worst reifications of oppressive structures that are constitutive of interpersonal violence.

• The racial dimensions of gender-based violence must always be addressed.

• Mass criminalization is gendered, a facet that is too often ignored.

• It is important to use a politics of collective, mass defense to challenge the intersections of gendered violence and racialized criminalization.

• Women and gender nonconforming people's rights to self-defense and self-determination must be won through popular support.

• Acts of self-defense are valid in order to affirm all women and gender nonconforming people's rights to bodily autonomy.

• It is critical to assert and preserve marginalized people's right to self-defense because we are both under-protected and targeted by the state and sometimes by our own communities.

• The violent/nonviolent offense binary is an insidious mirage, and we must fight for everyone's freedom. Petitioning the state that is set up to kill us for help and protection can be untenable and therefore forces us to consider new ways of seeking some justice.

• Criminalization itself is sexual violence—a form of state enactment of gendered violence—which is an important reason to oppose it.

- We cannot focus on addressing vulnerabilities through criminalization, which is always racialized, classed, gendered, and heteronormed. So a focus on criminalized survivors of violence pushes us to ask, "How do we create safety outside of carceral logics?"

In March 2015, I had the great honor to moderate a panel at the Color of Violence conference organized by INCITE! Women, Gender Nonconforming, and Trans People of Color Against Violence. The panel included formerly criminalized survivors of violence including Yvonne Wanrow, Marissa Alexander (appearing via Skype), CeCe McDonald, and Renata Hill. Former political prisoner Angela Davis sat in the front row of the audience.

The web of connections between these women was made visible as Marissa told a story of watching the documentary *Free Angela and All Political Prisoners* while on house arrest. She said that the film gave her strength that contributed to her survival. CeCe shared that she had a #FreeMarissa poster in her cell while incarcerated and that reading Davis's *Are Prisons Obsolete?* radicalized her while on the inside. Yvonne Wanrow thanked Angela Davis for contributing to her defense committee in the 1970s. The ethic and practice of abolitionist care links those criminalized to each other and also to us on the outside. Hundreds of us witnessed and understood the importance and value of defense campaigns that night.

A practice of decarcerality that intends to win must include fighting to free individuals from cages, and that must include fighting to defend and free criminalized survivors of violence. This will ensure that our movement for abolition is strengthened and can grow. Free Us All!*

* This essay benefitted greatly from feedback and edits by Alisa Bierria, Nancy Heitzeg, Colby Lenz, Erica Meiners, and Andy Smith. Sincere thanks for your suggestions and ideas.

Rekia Boyd and #FireDanteServin: An Abolitionist Campaign in Chicago

On Showing Up, Erasing Myself, and Lifting Up the Choir

Prison Culture, April 2015

It was unlikely that we would come to know her by her first name: Rekia. She was a twenty-two-year-old young Black woman when Dante Servin, a Chicago Police Department detective, shot her in the head. In the political economy of memorials and public grieving, being a young Black woman is not advantageous. The names that we lift up (when we memorialize Black lives at all) are usually attached to cis heterosexual men: Sean, Rodney, Amadou, Mike, Tamir, and now Freddie . . .

I was at the Nashville airport last Monday when my phone started ringing. Friends who were at Dante Servin's trial were calling and texting to relay the news. Judge Porter granted the defense's motion for a directed finding and dismissed the case against Servin. I was not surprised. I only felt sad for Rekia Boyd's family. They did not get the justice that they sought. They waited three years for Servin's day in court. They fought for over eighteen months just for an indictment. No cop had been tried for killing someone in Cook County for seventeen years. Then Dante Servin walked out of 26th and California a free man, ready to carry a gun and to patrol the streets again.

In Chicago, Servin's acquittal led to a couple of small, heartfelt protests and some limited outrage. A couple of weeks ago, I lamented how few people attended a rally on the first day of Dante Servin's trial. I can't lie. I was disappointed in the turnout. I know, I know that there are hundreds of reasons people didn't show up in numbers. A friend mentioned that perhaps the rain had kept them away. I stared at him. We both knew the truth. For all of the talk of Black lives mattering, all evidence points to the opposite. Rekia's life surely mattered to her family and friends. It matters to the small but determined group that showed up in solidarity with her family. Beyond that though, no, Rekia's life doesn't matter in this country.

There is in fact a hierarchy of oppression as Black women and Black trans and gender nonconforming people have even less access to limited sympathy than do cis heterosexual Black men. To deny this is to be a liar. When we call out, "Who will keep our sisters?" too often we are greeted with one or two lone voices in the wilderness but usually with silence.

Partly in response to my words and as a balm for my and others' demoralization, some friends and comrades organized a beautiful show of support and solidarity for Rekia. My friend Kelly, one of the organizers of the light action, wrote:

> Tonight, after a great deal of discussion and reflection, my friends and I decided to offer what we could to those who are mourning, discouraged, and in need of hope. We decided to offer a bit of light and action, in the hopes that seeing a message for Rekia projected in the night sky, in the heart of our city, might make them feel a little less disheartened, and a little less alone. It's a small offering, to be sure, but it is one that is made with love, and with a great deal of hope.

I was very moved by the light action. I have struggled for a couple of weeks to adequately convey my emotions. I found some words after reading a post titled "No One Showed Up to Rally for Rekia." While the title suggested an absence of people at the rally, the post began with this sentence: "Last night in New York City's Union Square, a modest crowd of between 30 and 50 people (depending on who you ask) showed up to rally for Rekia Boyd and Black women and girls who've been killed by police." So, in fact, some people (albeit a small number) did attend the rally.

The title of the post grated. I thought of those few dozen people who took the time to show up for Rekia and her family. Perhaps they were members of the choir so to speak but they were definitely somebody. One of the organizers of the rally noted on social media that she was frustrated that those people who did show up (mostly Black women) were being dismissed and overlooked. She suggested that this was both an erasure of Black women's labor as organizers and a discounting of the fact that we regularly show up for each other even when others do not for us. She was right on both counts.

I often remind others of the importance of lifting up the choir, of ensuring that those who do show up know that we are grateful for and value them. I've lectured others on the importance of never taking the choir for granted. Yet as I struggled with my demoralization, I disregarded my own admonition. Those of us who show up matter, and as Kelly has written: "What we are doing together matters, and must continue." In a sense, I had written myself out of the story of resistance against Rekia's killing. I had erased myself as a Black woman who shows up for other Black women across the spectrum and who understands that I cannot live without my life.

There is a lot of pain and anger about the invisibility of Black women, trans and gender nonconforming people in struggles against state and interpersonal violence. Rightly so. It hurts to be erased and overlooked. But it's important, I think, to simultaneously recognize those who do, in fact, insist on making these lives matter too. It's always both/and.

#FireDanteServin

Prison Culture, September 2015

When Judge Porter acquitted officer Dante Servin for killing Rekia Boyd, Martinez Sutton, Rekia's brother, was so gutted that he couldn't contain his pain. He and others in the courtroom were temporarily detained by police. Rekia's family, friends, and community were devastated. Dante Servin was free. How long before he might kill someone else? How long before the next Rekia? How long before Rekia's mother could finally sleep soundly through the night?

By all accounts, the prosecution's heart was not in the case. More than that, as most now understand, police officers are rarely indicted and almost never convicted.

Rekia was still dead, and Dante Servin still had his job and pension.

A couple of days later, about eleven people representing several organizations including Black Youth Project 100, Project NIA, Black

Lives Matter Chicago, Women's All Points Bulletin, Feminist Uprising to Resist Inequality and Exploitation, International Socialist Organization, We Charge Genocide, and Chicago Taskforce on Violence against Girls & Young Women met on the South Side to brainstorm and discuss next steps in the struggle for justice for Rekia. Those in attendance identified as abolitionists, progressives, socialists, and anarchists. Our goal was to develop a strategy to keep Rekia's name alive and to continue to support her family.

This didn't happen by chance. Her family and local organizers have insisted that her life mattered. The meeting we held after the Servin verdict was a declaration that Rekia would not be forgotten and that her family would not be abandoned.

By the end of the meeting, we had agreed to collectively organize several events and actions through the spring and summer. Groups and individuals volunteered to bottom-line several projects. Project NIA and the Taskforce on Violence against Girls & Young Women took responsibility for organizing a legal teach-in about the case that would take place the next week. That event sent DePaul Law School and the Chicago Police Department into a panic. On the heels of the Baltimore uprisings, they deployed dozens of police officers to surveil and monitor attendees. Project NIA also took responsibility for coordinating a month-long series of events under the banner of "Black August Chicago." These events, actions, and interventions would focus on state violence against Black women and girls (trans and non-trans) and contextualize these experiences historically. Most of the groups at the meeting committed to organize an event, action, or intervention during Black August.

BYP 100 committed to reach out to national groups to organize a National Day of Action for Black Women and Girls on May 21. BLM Chicago, We Charge Genocide, and WAPB decided to attend the next police board meeting to demand the firing of Dante Servin. Since that board meeting would be on May 21, it worked out that the BYP 100 National Day of Action for Black Women and Girls local event would dovetail with the effort to #FireDanteServin.

As a by-product of the community's organizing, the Independent Police Review Authority recommended the firing of Servin. CPD Superintendent McCarthy now has ninety days to offer his recommendation, which would then go to the Police Board for a final vote. So there are more steps and work ahead. In the meantime, the relationships between individuals and groups organizing to #FireDanteServin and against police violence more generally are deepening, and the number of people joining the mobilizations is growing.

There has been some criticism about the strategic value of a campaign focused on firing one police officer. Isn't this simply individualizing harm? Shouldn't we be taking a systemic, structural approach to addressing police violence?

None of the organizers leading the #FireServin actions believe that his dismissal from the force will end police violence. Servin is buttressed and backed by a culture of impunity and by a history of Black deathmaking in this city. He is one brick in a reinforced wall. Just a brick. Organizers know this. So why focus on Servin at all? I'll share some reasons below:

1) The demand to fire Servin is consistent with abolitionist goals in that it addresses the issue of accountability for harm caused.

2) The demand to fire Servin is in response to the desire of a devastated family and community to see a modicum of justice for their daughter, sister, friend, and fellow human being.

3) The demand to fire Servin exists within a broader set of mobilizations and actions that are about *making* all #BlackWomenAndGirlsLivesMatter.

4) The demand to fire Servin has an origin story rooted in collective brainstorming and organizing. It has provided a tangible way to build power through the mobilizations.

5) The demand to fire Servin has provided an opportunity for some individuals and groups to collaborate more closely and to get to know each other in ways that will only strengthen our broader local struggle. If we learn to fight together, we can win together.

6) The demand to fire Servin has not and does not preclude others from pursuing and taking on their own campaigns to end police

violence. Moreover, campaign organizers themselves are involved in more than just efforts to fire Servin.

In Rekia's name, organizers in Chicago have launched a sustained mobilization seeking justice for all Black women and girls. It's remarkable, really. All of the #SayHerName and #JusticeForRekia actions and mobilizations that happened across the country on May 21 had their roots here in Chicago. It has been rare in US history to effectively organize at the intersection of race and gender. Yet, in part because of our work seeking #JusticeForRekia, there is some energy behind a focus on state violence against all Black women and girls. And this matters a great deal. The recent attention paid to Sandra Bland, Natasha McKenna, and the ongoing killings of Black trans women is partly owed to this mobilization.

A focus on how women and girls experience violence by the state pushes us to consider more than lethal force as harmful. We have to consider sexual assaults by police (inside prisons and in the streets). We have to include how women who are victims of interpersonal violence are criminalized by the state for defending their lives. Our lens becomes wider. Hence, the #FireDanteServin campaign has not simply been about holding one officer accountable. It's also been about making visible the neglected forms of violence experienced by Black women and girls across this country and beyond.

Four Years since a Chicago Police Officer Killed Rekia Boyd, Justice Still Hasn't Been Served

In These Times, March 2016

The fact that Rekia Boyd's name might be familiar to you is a testament to her family and local Chicago activists' persistent and effective organizing. Today marks four years since detective Dante Servin killed Rekia in the North Lawndale neighborhood. She was unarmed and hanging out with friends when Servin shot her in the head. He was off-duty and carrying an unregistered gun at the time.

Servin is the very rare police officer who was actually tried for the extrajudicial killing of an unarmed Black person. In fact, prior to him, it had been seventeen years since a cop was tried for killing someone in Cook County. A Servin conviction would have been shocking.

But he was not convicted. In April 2015, Judge Porter dismissed all charges against him essentially on a technicality, suggesting that the prosecution had mischarged the officer.

Rekia's family and their supporters were understandably angry. Martinez Sutton, Rekia's brother, shouted in court when the judge issued his decision: "You want me to be quiet? This motherfucker killed my sister!" Martinez along with other supporters was dragged out of the proceedings by deputies. Dante Servin walked out of court a free man, allowed to carry a gun and to patrol the streets again.

Over the past four years, the indignities have piled up. Rekia's family and community fought for over eighteen months to get an indictment of Servin by Cook County State's Attorney Anita Alvarez. They waited three years for Servin's day in court. They did not get the justice that they sought. Yet rather than dampening their spirits, Servin's acquittal galvanized Chicago activists and organizers who have rallied behind the demand to #FireDanteServin.

Since May 2015, Chicagoans have packed police board meetings to call for Dante Servin's termination without pension from the Chicago Police Department. Firing a CPD officer is a three-step process. In September 2015, after a lengthy investigation, the Independent Police Review Authority recommended that Servin be fired. Then in November, former police superintendent Garry McCarthy concurred. The last step in the process is a hearing set for May 2016 before the police board after which a final decision on his employment status will be rendered.

Rekia's name and her story have been uplifted in the many #BlackLivesMatter actions and protests taking place across Chicago and the country. At last October's International Association of Chiefs of Police Conference in Chicago, for example, a group of women and gender nonconforming people of color shut down access to McCormick Place where thousands of law enforcement officials from around the world were gathered. The protesters wore T-shirts emblazoned with Rekia's image. It was more than a symbolic gesture or simple commemoration: it was a statement that Rekia is not forgotten and that her spirit lives in current organizing and protests.

Alvarez was defeated in a Democratic primary in her attempt to win a third term in office. Her defeat can in large part by blamed on her handling of police violence cases including Rekia's. Rekia's name and story were consistently raised during the direct actions that targeted Alvarez through the #ByeAnita campaign. Writing on Facebook a couple of days before the primary, Assata's Daughters, a key organization in the #ByeAnita campaign, explicitly cited Rekia as an inspiration: "The message is "Vote Out Anita" but the reason is We <3 Laquan and We <3 Rekia. All of this has been for them. Literally blood, sweat, and tears have been poured into this campaign."

There are countless stories of women and gender nonconforming people who have experienced police violence. Yet, as political theorist Dr. Joy James has written: "The death of women in police custody by means of law enforcement measures to discipline and punish is an issue rarely raised in feminist explorations of women and violence or masculinist explorations of racism and policing." Recently however, through the #SayHerName mobilizations, more women and gender nonconforming victims and survivors of state violence are being made visible. Visibility is a necessary precursor to accountability. This is in part of Rekia's legacy.

At trial in April 2015, Rekia's close friend Ikca testified that once Dante Servin began shooting, all who were gathered ran from his bullets. Ikca hid behind a large tree to avoid being shot. She saw Rekia on the ground injured and dying. Ikca was prevented from riding with Rekia in the ambulance. In fact, the police at the scene threatened to arrest her if she didn't leave. Ikca told the judge that Rekia hated to be alone.

As we mark the fourth anniversary of Rekia's tragic killing, her family, friends and community are still mourning her loss and are more determined than ever to win a modicum of justice for her. Rekia is not alone. She has a community of thousands fighting against state violence in her name and memory.

Rest in peace, Rekia. Rest in power.

A Love Letter to the #NoCopAcademy* Organizers from Those of Us on the Freedom Side

Prison Culture, March 2019

You fought hard, and the entrenched corrupt interests in Chicago still decided to back an unnecessary and inherently violent police "training" facility, to be built on the West Side of the city. How tired you must be feeling after all of these months of struggle. Perhaps some of you are even wondering this evening whether your organizing was worth the time, energy, heart, and spirit you devoted to it. After all, the City Council's vote is one you didn't want to see happen. You were hoping for a different outcome.

So isn't this a loss? Didn't you fail to win? A surface assessment of the campaign would say that the answer is yes. But you have been strategic, thoughtful, and critical throughout this campaign, so I know that you know surface assessments are not the full story. They are not *the* truth. *Organizing is mostly about defeats.* Often when we engage in campaigns, we lose. But any organizer worth their salt knows that it's much more complex than a simple win-lose calculus.

Here's what I know. Rahm and his cronies were hoping to ram through a proposal for a $95 million police training academy under the cover of darkness with no community input. A group made up mostly of young Black and brown people decided that this was wrong for a num-

---

* The No Cop Academy campaign, supported by over eighty community organizations, was launched in 2017 to oppose then Chicago mayor Rahm Emanuel's proposal for establishing a police and fire training academy in a Black community on the city's West Side. Elected as the mayor of Chicago in 2019, Lori Lightfoot supports the building of the academy.

ber of reasons. You then spent the better part of eighteen months *showing* people in Chicago and beyond through your actions that the power structure in the city would be in for a titanic fight to resist their plans. How did you do this? You researched their plans and proposals, you learned about zoning laws on the fly, you litigated when you were excluded from public meetings, you mobilized thousands, you engaged in political education, you developed the leadership of hundreds of new young organizers, you truly centered the ideas of young people of color, you conducted participatory action research, and you *shut shit down*. Through your actions, people quite literally the world over expressed their solidarity with your fight. They saw themselves as directly implicated in the vision of the world you have so beautifully inhabited all these months. All of these are wins.

Even if I didn't know many of you personally, I would be in awe of what you did. But because I know many of you, I feel even more admiration because I know what you've sacrificed to wage this fight. I know about long strategy sessions, missed weekend relaxation, moments of doubt, and most of all consistent commitment.

#NoCopAcademy is an abolitionist organizing campaign, and through your work you've helped others understand what it means when we say that abolition is a practical organizing strategy. You told a story about policing as an inherently violent and deathmaking institution that *will not* be reformed by training cops better or in fancier digs. You pointed out all of the resources that this cop academy will swallow up and told the city that those resources should be diverted to life-giving institutions. You asked the right questions, like: "Why are we feeding an institution that leads to the premature death of so many Black and brown people (especially young ones)?"

The responses that you got were inadequate. Your opponents were exposed as uninformed, corrupt, and craven. You embodied #NoCop-Academy organizer Benji Hart's analysis of abolition as a way "to transform our reactions to individual traumatic events into codified political commitments." You showed that abolition as a project is about building a vision of a different world: one where everyone has their needs met and where #BlackLivesMatter.

There are people, and perhaps some of you are among them, who are asking, "What now?" For the core organizers of this campaign,

abolition is becoming a slightly more popular idea, more now identify as PIC abolitionists. We consider this a positive development for the most part. But what should we make of "abolitionist" declarations of support for R. Kelly's imprisonment? What do they mean? How can self-professed PIC abolitionists also rejoice in the caging of fellow human beings?

Being personally thrilled with someone going to prison is anyone's prerogative, and we understand that a person may feel joy at another's incapacitation if that individual has repeatedly and unrepentantly caused grievous harm. Let's be clear though: advocating for someone's imprisonment is not abolitionist. Mistaking emotional satisfaction for justice is also not abolitionist.

Abolitionism is not a politics mediated by emotional responses. Or, as we initially wanted to title this piece, abolition is not about your fucking feelings. Of course, everything involves feelings, but celebrating anyone's incarceration is counter to PIC abolition.

This may frustrate or anger people who want to claim an abolitionist identity or politic despite not being ready to operate from basic abolitionist principles. We understand. For years, both of us have facilitated community accountability processes to address interpersonal harms (particularly involving sexual and intimate partner violence). As survivors of sexual harm, accountability is always at the forefront in our consciousness. We understand how damaging and serious sexual violence is. And we too have sometimes wished that abolition wasn't so rigorous in its demands of our politics.

While abolition is a flexible praxis contingent upon social conditions and communal needs, it is built on a set of core principles. Everyone doesn't have to be an abolitionist. But if you declare yourself to be, you're committing to some basic obligations, including a few below that we've identified through study and practice:

• Prison-industrial complex abolition calls for the elimination of policing, imprisonment, and surveillance.

• PIC abolition rejects the expansion in breadth or scope or legitimation of all aspects of the prison-industrial complex—surveillance, policing, sentencing, and imprisonment of all sorts.

• PIC abolition refuses premature death and organized abandonment, the state's modes of reprisal and punishment.

These principles matter. One may advocate for radical reform of surveillance, policing, sentencing, and imprisonment without defining oneself as a prison abolitionist. We feel that this may need to be explicitly stated in this current historical moment. Abolitionists often do propose and organize around radical reforms that we hope will lead us toward a future free of the prison-industrial complex. However, not everyone who organizes for radical reforms is a PIC abolitionist. That's more than okay. In any movement for change, there will be multiple theories and visions. But a commitment to the principles of prison abolition is incompatible with the idea that incarceration is a just or appropriate solution for interpersonal harms—*ever*.

As PIC abolitionists and transformative justice practitioners, we're always asked, "What about the rapists?" Lately, the question has been phrased like this: "Well, surely you don't mean that R. Kelly shouldn't be in prison?" We do.

What we tell people is this: the criminal legal system will never "bring to justice" every person who does harm in our society. This is impossible. We cannot under any system "prosecute" our way out of harm. As a strategy for justly evaluating and adjudicating sexual harm, the criminal legal system has proven, empirically and qualitatively, an utter failure. Relying on it as the sole response to sexual violence has failed to offer opportunities for accountability and healing for those directly impacted by that violence; in fact, the criminal legal system does not even purport to care about whether survivors of sexual violence heal. Billions of dollars are poured yearly into a criminal legal system most people involved in proceedings of say doesn't deliver the justice they seek.

The onus is not on the system's critics to defend our position. There is already plenty of evidence. The answers for what we should do about R. Kelly are many, but they must be collectively determined by our communities. PIC abolition offers both a framework for a much-needed structural analysis of the world and a practical organizing strategy to transform it. The criminal legal system, for example, focuses on punishing or disempowering individual "offenders" who have done harm. PIC abolitionists, however, consider the larger social, economic, and political context in which the harm occurs.

In the case of Kelly, what accountability do we attribute to the record executives propping up and facilitating his ability to harm people? Should they also be prevented from exercising power within the recording industry? Should Kelly and the record executives attached to him be prevented from ever benefitting financially from the recording industry moving forward?

Having determined a need for accountability, we must consider a range of alternatives for redress. Sometimes we demand concrete restitution that supports survivor and community healing. Other times, we insist on counseling and other interventions that can produce changes in behavior.

We also can't discuss alternative ways of addressing harm in a vacuum. We have to ask how the current system evaluates and adjudicates harms. In 2019, when we ask what should be done about Kelly, we must acknowledge the social context. For example, the current president of the United States has been accused by more than twenty people of sexual assault and rape. Even after the release of archival video in which he freely admitted to sexually assaulting women, tens of millions of people voted to install him as president. In the past few years, the #MeToo movement has emboldened survivors to share stories of their experiences of harm and survivorship at the hands of politically and socially powerful men, in part because of the message they have received that legal redress is possible—as is supposedly illustrated by the high-profile trials of Bill Cosby and the upcoming trial of Harvey Weinstein.

But the power dynamics that create the conditions that fuel sexual violence go unaddressed and are even maintained by criminal legal proceedings. For example, "Emily Doe," who survived rape at the hands of Brock Turner, described in a victim impact statement for the high-profile trial in Palo Alto, California, the additional violence she experienced through the process of the trial. In her statement she says,

> After a physical assault, I was assaulted with questions designed to attack me, to say see, her facts don't line up, she's out of her mind, she's

practically an alcoholic, she probably wanted to hook up, he's like an athlete right, they were both drunk, whatever, the hospital stuff she remembers is after the fact, why take it into account, Brock has a lot at stake so he's having a really hard time right now.

In light of the failures of the criminal legal system, why would system defenders and reformers fear experiments or different structures for addressing harm? What could be lost by expanding the range of remedies available to us? While critics of the system may not need to defend the desire for expanded remedies, we do need to try our best to reduce suffering and not to compound the existing harms.

As Aurora Levins Morales teaches us, "The stories we tell about our suffering define what we can imagine doing about it." Currently the prevailing story told about sexual violence is that our suffering can be fixed by the criminal legal system. Legal remedies such as restraining orders and criminal charges are the primary forms of redress offered to survivors of violence and harm. This limited range of remedies frequently forecloses our consideration of other possible ways to address sexual harm. Abolition is the praxis that gives us room for new visions and allows us to write new stories—together. But it is hard, hard work.

Abolition forecasts a world not yet realized, but some self-proclaimed abolitionists seem to believe that we have already failed. They have suggested that abolitionist responses failed to stop Kelly and are therefore failures. (These critics also tend to use *abolition* and *transformative justice* interchangeably.) They are inventing a past that never was: what range of abolitionist alternatives do we imagine was offered to survivors of Kelly's harm? As we've just noted, survivors are offered a very limited set of responses through the criminal legal system. And anything beyond these systems-based approaches is usually painted as too risky or irresponsible to pursue. Further, framing transformative justice as an alternative to imprisonment demonstrates a gross misunderstanding of the concept. Transformative justice is a framework that can only be applied responsibly in relationship to the specific context in which it is being practiced. It's not a one-to-one replacement for criminal legal punishment and should not be thought of as a stand-in.

There is another problem with this predictive rhetoric of failure: it suggests that abolitionists believe that there should be no consequences for harm. "If you don't believe that it's appropriate to lock human beings in cages, then you must think nothing should happen to people who harm others," claim these detractors. And this is the very heart of the problem: it's prison or nothing. While abolitionists hold a range of values, principles, and ideas about transformation, we've never known an abolitionist who thought that nothing was the preferred alternative to imprisonment. We believe in consequences for harm, for Kelly or anyone else.

Those consequences may involve forgoing royalties and any future financial gain derived from the context in which the harm occurred, or being required to pay restitution or provide labor to those who have been harmed, their families, and, when appropriate, their communities. Those consequences might include restricted access to specific groups or spaces, or ineligibility for positions of leadership. Consequences might also include being required to make a public apology. Regardless of what's chosen, the point is that any consequences should be determined in direct relationship to the harm done and should involve input by people impacted by the harm.

The idea that until abolitionist approaches can meet people's idealized version of an appropriate response, prison is the best solution is, at best, a failure of imagination and a manifestation of blinkered thinking. It suggests that PIC abolition is some fixed horizon at which we will arrive without having to put in any effort. But there will never be a day when the skies open up and the angels sing, "Abolition!"

The conditions in which abolitionist approaches will flourish won't magically appear. They must be fought for and nurtured and defended. For those conditions to exist, we need to put in the steady work of eliminating the use of surveillance, policing, sentencing, and imprisonment. For those conditions to exist, we need to practice operating without using those systems and institutions. For those conditions to exist, we must create them. Acceding, as some do, to "prison in the meantime" only prevents them from taking root.

Abolition is not about your feelings. It is not about emotional satisfaction. It's about transforming the conditions in which we live, work, and play such that harm at the scale and as prolonged as that perpetrated by R. Kelly cannot develop and cannot be sustained. But you can put your feelings to work in fighting for PIC abolition. If you do, you should be warned, however, there will be no magical day of liberation that we do not make. What or who are these other self-proclaimed abolitionists waiting for? The time is now.

The Practices We Need:
#MeToo and Transformative Justice

Interview by Autumn Brown and adrienne maree brown

How to Survive the End of the World, November 2018

adrienne maree brown: *The #MeToo movement has swollen and become this massive place where a lot of people are calling for transformative justice and community accountability processes, and I'm wondering how you see it.*

Mariame Kaba: Yeah, I have been thinking a lot about #MeToo and thinking, What if we look at it as something that is not done to "bad people?" What if it is actually a way to understand the ways that various forms of violence actually shape our lives? If we could see it as a way to understand how deeply enmeshed we are in the very systems that we're organizing to transform, then I feel like it's a movement that will allow us to move a step toward transformation and more justice. The real truth of the matter is that when you think about #MeToo and you think about sexual violence, these things don't live outside of us. They really don't. They are systems that live within us, that manifest outside of us. If we don't really take that seriously, I don't think we're going to make a dent in this problem.

The fact that sexual violence is so incredibly pervasive should tell us that it's not a story of individual monsters. We have got to think about this in a more complex way if we're really going to uproot forms of sexual violence.

Autumn Brown: *If you could, say more about what you mean by "these systems live inside us as well as outside of us."*

Kaba: This is something I take from Morgan Bassichis, who was part

139

of Oakland-based Community United Against Violence. Morgan had written that basically the very systems that we're working to dismantle live inside us. And that really struck me when I first read it. It forced me to acknowledge my own complicity in forms of violence that I may not even personally be perpetrating in an intentional way. It also calmed me down to some extent. When you're always in a position of seeing everything as outside of you, then you're always on the outside looking in, which isn't necessarily the best way to address forms of violence. We have to do both. We have to be on the outside looking in but also on the inside looking out.

Brown: *When and where in your trajectory in this work did you really decide to start focusing on working with those who have caused harm. And how did that happen for you?*

Kaba: I've always worked more with people who have been harmed than have caused harm. My work was rooted in supporting survivors, mainly because I myself am one. And my orientation has always been toward addressing harm, wherever it is. However I can intervene in a way that's supportive, that's really what I care about. It didn't really matter whether it was the person who caused harm or the person who has experienced harm—it's the harm that I'm interested in transforming.

Over the years more people started approaching me. Initially I got called into this work by happenstance. A friend of mine was sexually assaulted in the early 2000s by somebody else that we knew in common. And I was called in to help and to support her through that process. I didn't ask to do this. And still, I'm not paid to do this kind of work. I facilitate only within my communities. So it became something where it was like, "Oh, I'm going to try to step in and support these folks who I know. And I don't want the harm to compound. And clearly people are in pain. And what can I help do to support that?"

I'm not trained as a social worker or a psychologist or anything like that. It was really like, "This is happening in my community, people are in pain, there's harm, what can we do." About fifteen years ago people started asking me to come and support them. Come and help. People who caused harm reached out and said, "This has occurred, and I'm trying to figure out what to do." That's how that happened. And then in the last few years a couple of processes that I facilitated got known by other people. And through that more people who have caused harm approached me. Or people who knew people who had caused harm would approach me to support them in taking accountability for their actions.

Note that I said support them in taking accountability for their actions. I'm not able to actually force anybody into taking accountability. It has to be a voluntary process through which somebody decides to do that. You can never actually make anybody accountable. People have to be accountable. I want to be very explicit about that. A lot of the frustration that I hear from people who think about transformative justice or community accountability is really people who want to punish people. I totally understand that they want punishment. It's a normal human reaction within a society that is so incredibly punitive. How do you live outside that?

Remember again, the systems live within us. The punishment mindset is very hard to get out of. And it's normal and healthy often to want vengeance against people for causing you great harm. That's not going to get addressed in an accountability process. If you are the one who is rushing after that and that's really what you're seeking, an accountability process really would not help. You're always going to be feeling as though it's "not working" because it's not doing the thing that you really would like.

And I really want to make people understand that. Not everything should be in an accountability process. Not everything can be resolved in an accountability process. Accountability processes often feel terrible to the people while they're in it. It's not a healing process. It might put you on the road toward your own personal healing.

Brown: *This is exactly where we're heading. This is exactly what we want to get into. The experience I have as someone who is trying to mediate things is that people go through it, they go through one time, the process doesn't work the way they want it to. They don't feel like we deeply returned to a place of love that we had never reached in the first place: we're totally healed, it's all clear. We don't get that. And then people are like, "Well, transformative justice doesn't work. Fuck this process, I'm not going to do it." . . . what are some of the other things that make it fail, and then, conversely, what are some of the things that make it succeed?*

Kaba: While the person has to be willing to at least begin a process of taking accountability for their actions, they don't need to necessarily be at the point where they've admitted harm. I think this is very important. Because what is the process for? It's to get people to understand how they've harmed people. It's to get them to sit with this harm that happened to this person and to be like, "Oh my god, I thought I was doing this right thing, and here's this situation, and this is the person's experience." So I think often people think before we can even start a process people have to put out a statement. Well, no, the statement process writing thing might be part of the accountability process, but it's not necessarily necessary for the beginning of it, in order to initiate it. So that's very important for people to understand off the bat.

I want to say something also briefly about the concept of success and failure. In trainings that I do with my good friend Shira Hassan we read a very short piece that was written by Bench Ansfield and Jenna Peters-Golden about getting seduced by the idea of success and failure within processes, published in in *Makeshift,* a feminist magazine. And it's really helpful. Failure and mistakes are part of a process. That feels counterintuitive because when people are in pain and have been harmed, you think you have to be perfect in order to protect that person from further harm. And what I always tell people is that as a survivor and as somebody who has been around survivors my entire life in my community, we are actually not fragile beings. We are incredibly, incredibly pragmatic. And very resilient. Because we've survived a lot of bullshit.

And so going into processes, if you go into it with an idea that the person you're working with is a fragile China doll who is going to crack under any pressure, you can't make a mistake—well, then you're already set up for failure, in the sense of potential catastrophic hurt. Start off with the notion that our process allows for survivors to reclaim agency. That's what you're working toward. The binary of success/failure, get rid of that. That's important, number one.

Number two, you have to know the goals of the process. A third thing is knowing whether or not you're the right person to actually get into this. Do you have the support system that will help you navigate this? Are you facilitating this by yourself? Do you have a team of people? How are you going to end this process? Because it should not be something that goes on for ninety years. There should be an end to it. How will you know it is over? Having goals will help you in that. So those are all very critical important things to have at the outset or to be working out through the process. I think the failure parts or the places that will ensure ineffectiveness are not knowing whether or not you're the right person to hold this.

It's not having any goals. It's the other side of the thing I just said are the ingredients that you need for a strong process. It's really not being clear with people about what the wants and needs are. What do people really want? And you can't get—people cannot get all their wants met in a process.

Brown: *Just as a follow-up to that, are there processes that you're like, "I feel like I have to walk away from this"? And are there processes that you've heard that you're like, "Oh, I know what to offer." Do you only respond if people are like, "Come help," or are there things where you're like, "Hey, I see y'all over there?"*

Kaba: I never seek out any processes. Ever. It's not a job for me. It's not a way of sustenance. It's a political commitment that I make because I'm in community with people who aren't going to avail themselves of the systems that currently exist for multiple reasons. And it also fits within my larger political commitment to PIC abolition. That is why I'm engaged. I never seek out any processes; people come to me. Frankly much more than I can even offer any support around. But I'm very good about boundaries. I'm very good about confining myself to what I really think I can offer. I'm one person. There's no way I can have integrity and give what needs to be done to everything if I'm just all over the place. I really focus on that. And I always tell people where I stand. And sometimes I can try to help people figure out whether a process is possible, so I might do that. So those are the kinds of things I would do.

Brown: *And what I hear in what you're describing is the difference between intervention versus support. Right. That in our movement spaces we do need those kinds of interventions of, "Hey, y'all, take this offline." This is not the way that we're going to get healing or accountability. But I'm hearing the difference between those kinds of interventions versus what level of commit-*

ment is required in order to be a part of a sustained process. . . . I personally really struggle with this question of what is the relationship between healing and accountability? Especially coming out of a healing justice framework in terms of my movement background.

Kaba: Yes, this is a great question. I'm going to backtrack one second to the question of intervention versus support. I also think we need to make distinctions between conflict resolution and accountability processes. I think that's right. And I think I'm not an expert in conflict resolution, actually. I've never taken a class. I don't know how to—that's not the work I do. I help some people facilitate processes of accountability, which is different. And so I think sometimes we're all over the place in our language. But that also leads to people thinking they're doing everything, and then they're doing nothing. I think that's important to keep in mind.

So, jumping to the question that you actually asked about healing, I think it's such an important question. I've come to my understanding of this through being part of processes. Initially I thought that these processes were intended for healing. But it turned out that I wasn't actually asking the people involved what their needs and wants were. And for many people it was not actually healing. They were not trying—their needs were not to heal within this particular space. Their needs were to have an acknowledgement of the harm that occurred, to insist that this person never do this again, to address issues around trust and figuring out how to trust people again. It was self-agency and self-accountability. There was a list of things. And healing almost never came up. So that sounds a bit counterintuitive. But I realized later on why that was. And it was because people were actually understanding that to heal, they needed a different kind of space to be in.

They were initially coming to me at a point where it was high amounts of pain, suffering, lots of emotions happening. So much stuff happening that healing wasn't even in their head at the moment. It was like, "I'm just trying to maintain." This is going to help me get to the point where I can feel like I can be in my apartment by myself again. I need people around me to do that, so how am I going to get my friends on board with coming and visiting me every week? Things like that were what was needed to get on the path toward their own very long journey toward a healing space. But it wasn't a destination within the process itself. And that helped me figure out later on when people would say, "I didn't get healing," I was like, "Oh, okay." I was hearing other people say, "The process was really traumatic for me. It brought up all this stuff for me. It was painful for me. It was whatever." And people were like, "Oh, that meant that it was ineffective and that it was failing." And I was like actually in hearing how people were talking about that, I was like, "Actually this process sounds like it was doing exactly what was needed to get this person, a year down the road, toward their own healing." Figuring out what that would look like. I'm not saying that you won't necessarily get what you need to heal in a process. I'm just saying that for many, many times, processes feel terrible. Because the harm is so central. And if you're engaged in the process with the person who harmed you—my god. It's bringing up so much stuff that if you're constantly trying to grab at the healing, you're not in the harm, processing that. You're outside looking for that destination that's somewhere down the road. But no, actually we have to be right here right now, handling all that. The fear, the anger, the vengeance feelings, the back and forth sliding against one day you want them dead, the next day you're okay. We just have to be here holding this right now. So that's what I mean by it's not—often feels like it's not—a healing space. Because healed is not a destination. You're just always in process. So that's what I'm talking about. Doesn't mean that what you experience can't help toward that healing. Of course, it does in its best way, in its best iteration. But while you're in it, it often does not feel that way at all.

Brown: *I'm just wondering if you can talk about how doing this work has been transformational for you and how it's—if and how—it's changed your relationship to your own history.*

Kaba: Yes. Oh my gosh. Thank you for that question. Because I really wouldn't be doing this only as a political project if it wasn't also transforming me in the process of doing this work with other people. My friend Danielle Sered has said and written this thing that really made a difference for me. She's lovely and runs this organization here in New York called Common Justice, which people should look up for multiple reasons. But she wrote a thing that stuck with me, which was that "no one enters violence for the first time by committing it." No one enters violence for the first time by committing it. And it just—I was like—Jesus Christ. If that's true, then all this shit that we talk about, these binaries about victims and perpetrators—that explodes it all.

At heart it's the harm that exists that has motivated and transformed us and allowed us to continue, and if we're not intervened with, will keep harming people in bigger and bigger ways. When we know we're all going to harm each other, it's a matter of degrees.

So being in this work with people has helped to make what Sered said come to life for me in a way that just undergirds my values and my beliefs. In real, real ways. The second thing that I've learned about myself is how much I realize that punishment does not work. It does not work. If it actually did what people wanted, we'd be in a whole different place.

Not only is it true that punishment doesn't work, but also when you prioritize punishment it means that patriarchy remains firmly in place. And if I am at my core interested in dismantling systems of oppression, I have got to get rid of punishment. I have got to do it. But I want accountability. I want people to take responsibility. I want that internal resource that allows you to take responsibility for harms that you commit against yourself and other people. I want that to be a central part of how we interact with each other. Because while I don't believe in punishment, I believe in consequences for actions that are done to harm other people. I do. I think boundaries are important. I think all these things are really important. But with punishment at the center of everything we haven't been able to really address the other stuff that needs to happen. Because people fucking need to—they need to take accountability when they harm people.

brown: *Can I just ask a quick follow-up to that? Can you just give for our listeners and for us an example of a punishment versus a consequence?*

Kaba: Yes. Sure. Punishment means inflicting cruelty and suffering on people. When you are expecting consequences, those can be unpleasant and uncomfortable. But they are not suffering and inflicting pain on people and you want them to suffer as a result. That is different. And what I mean by that is, for example, powerful people stepping down from their jobs are consequences, not punishments. Why? Because we should have boundaries. And because shit that you did was wrong, and you having power is a privilege. That means we can take that away from you. You don't have power anymore. But if we were punishing you, we would make it so that you could never make a living again in any context, at any point. That's inflicting cruelty, suffering, and making it so that people cannot actually live a life. They can't access the basic things to make life livable.

If you are doing that to somebody, you're punishing them. If you are asking somebody to move to another place because they caused harm to the people living there: consequence. If you're making it so that person can never have housing: punishment. Okay, so you have to just be able to see the difference between inflicting cruelty, pain, and suffering and being uncomfortable and losing some privileges—these are not the same things.

Moving Past Punishment

Interview by Ayana Young

For the Wild, December 2019

Ayana Young: *I know that restorative justice and transformative justice are often conflated. To begin, I'm hoping we can differentiate the two.*

Mariame Kaba: Sure. I like to make sure that people really understand that restorative justice is how I came to gain an understanding of a possibility of repairing harm. I started thinking about restorative justice before I took on really thinking about PIC abolition, prison-industrial complex abolition. My interest in restorative justice predates my politic around prison-industrial complex abolition. While restorative justice has been picked up much more fully since I started getting trained in the mid-1990s, and in some ways has been co-opted by the system, the roots of restorative justice are still incredibly useful and valid.

Restorative justice is focused on the importance of relationships. It is focused on the importance of repair when those relationships are broken, when violations occur in our relationships. It is very much interested in community, because it asks whose responsibility is it to actually meet the obligations and needs that are created through violation? It asks the community to step in fully, to be less of a bystander and more of an actor in trying to repair harm. And finally, it's very much a framework and an ideology and a way of living that is interested in making sure that we remain in right relationship with each other, with the land, with the environment. So that's an expansive view of restorative justice.

Over the years, people have focused very much on an individualistic model of addressing harm, using restorative justice modalities and restorative justice practices. Among those are people who will often say

148

things like, "I'm running a circle, therefore I'm doing restorative justice." That is ridiculous. It's just a tool that people use within a larger framework of restorative justice, which asks people different kinds of questions. I like to not fall into binaries too much, like it's this or this. It's many different kinds of things to many different kinds of people who use it many different kinds of ways. How I came to focus on transformative justice really was that.

Transformative justice takes as a starting point the idea that what happens in our interpersonal relationships is mirrored and reinforced by the larger systems. If you can't think all the time about the interplay between those spheres, you end up too focused on the interpersonal, and therefore you cannot transform the conditions that led to the interpersonal harm and violence that you're dealing with at the moment. I like it because it feels like a more expansive framework and ideology than restorative justice as it's currently being practiced. The histories of both frameworks are just different. They come from different places. They come out of different communities, even if there are overlaps. And I think it's important always to think about where things come from and where things are rooted in order to understand what they are.

For me, transformative justice is about trying to figure out how we respond to violence and harm in a way that doesn't cause more violence and harm. It's asking us to respond in ways that don't rely on the state or social services necessarily if people don't want it. It is focusing on the things that we have to cultivate so that we can prevent future harm. Transformative justice is militantly against the dichotomies between victims and perpetrators, because the world is more complex than that: in a particular situation we're victimized, and in other situations we're the people that perpetrate harm. We have to be able to hold all those things together.

Young: *Thank you so much for explaining that in such depth. Now in thinking about the carceral state it becomes clear how perverse the system is. And that's not just in context to the ways in which we define justice through a punitive lens, but also the policies and culture within prison and our growing obsession with detention facilities.... I'd like to ask you about where you see this urge for punishment stemming from?*

Kaba: Often people think of punishment as rooted within religion. Many forms of religion talk about punishment and vengeance that various gods wreak. There's such a long history in terms of people's thinking about punishment. Brett Story's *Prison Land* makes the case that prisons, rather than coming from our desire for punishment, are actually instruments to punish. They create punishment. It's an issue of directionality, whether it is our thoughts around punishment and vengeance drive the making of the prison or if it's the other way around. The institutions create and reinforce punishment, in and of themselves.

It's been making me think anew about how punishment works or doesn't work. I have always maintained that, as human beings, when we are hurt, often we turn to wanting to hurt back. We spend a lot of time thinking about retribution and vengeance because that is conditioned in us, both, as I mentioned, through religion and through how we grew up in the culture and through how we think about being in right relationship again with each other.

Punishment feels like a necessary ingredient toward being able to get back to right relationship in some way. And transformative justice challenges those values quite a bit. And it's hard to hold. I too am conditioned in this culture and was punished myself as a child. Very hard to think of what else to do when violence or harm occurs in the world but to punish. It permeates so much that when somebody chooses to do something else, we sometimes react violently toward that person who doesn't choose to punish, who says actually I want to try a different way. Then it's like, "You aren't holding up your end of the bargain here. What are you saying about my values if you refuse to go after this person in a punishing way?" It's really complex. It's really complicated. It's something I do think a lot about on a regular basis. I'm working actually currently on a resource. It's tentatively titled "Interrupting the Punishment Mind-set," and it's intended to be a resource for teachers to work with younger people and help them to think about punishment differently, to move from a focus on punishment to a focus on accountability and consequences. I've been working on it for a long time now. And it's been a struggle because it's so hard to find materials that are the opposite of the thing that we do, which is to punish.

Young: *Much of your work challenges us to reframe our understanding of* *perpetrators of violence as well as, to some extent, violence itself. And approximately half of the people currently imprisoned in the US are serving sentences for violent crimes. It feels obvious that we need to talk about how and why violence is being used in our society and how we should contextualize violence more broadly. And then within that, how does this reframing aid us in understanding what has been referred to as the abuse-to-prison pipeline?*

Kaba: One of the things I want to say up front is that when you are a victim or a survivor, however you feel that you want to identify, it is painful to be victimized. It is painful to be a recipient of any form of violence. We have to acknowledge that up front. Whatever I say is not in any way to minimize the experience of violence. I myself have been a victim and a survivor of violence. I feel very specifically on a regular basis that I want to always uplift the harm that's caused and not minimize that in any way.

It is true that half the people who are currently incarcerated in our state prisons are there for violent crimes of some sort. That's complicated because what gets termed as violence reflects judgments and political decisions and don't get applied equally. I've been thinking quite a bit about what it means to use violence and what it means to be violent. A lot of times people who cause inordinate harm are not considered to be violent people, like people who are polluting our rivers through toxic waste and corporate crimes.

People who are sending thousands of people off to kill other people in wars all around the world are not considered criminal. We barely talk about the military-industrial complex as a form of violence that we need to be accountable for in some way. People who are on the antiwar side try to make that case and are very much drowned out by people who don't consider those things violent because for them, they may consider it "self-defense" or righteous or any sort of kind of thing. But I want to hold those up because those harm millions of people. In real ways. Yet when Johnny down the street takes a gun and shoots another person, that's held up as the pinnacle of violence, so we ought to lock Johnny up, or worse kill Johnny under the state's auspices of capital punishment.

Young: *I'd love for us to transition into a conversation around how our current policy and movements are being formed. Which is to say that they sometimes stem from very strong and powerful, albeit individual, voices. This topic feels especially difficult because there should never be an intent to negate any survivor's desire to see justice. But at the same time, it feels really irresponsible to apply one's personal quest for justice to an entire population as a standard. So where is the balance between having policy and response that is both less personal but is still informed by survivors?*

Kaba: Oh my gosh. You're asking me great hard questions. I keep threatening to write an essay called "Abolition Is Not About Your Fucking Feelings." I wrote that in a tweet and got so much blowback because people felt like I was insulting their ability to feel what they want to feel. That's really not what I'm saying. The concept of the personal being political as a basis for feminist organizing in the past is so true, and yet it is so fraught at the same time. What it's not saying—and I think what sometimes people want it to be saying—is that how I personally feel then should be made into policy. And we can't operate in a world where that's true. We shouldn't codify our personal feelings of vengeance to apply to the entire world.

You find the criminal punishment system has all these contradictions. Because on the one hand, the state sets itself up as the ultimate arbiter of "fighting for the victims." But nowhere in those proceedings is the "victim's" real interest. If the victim doesn't agree, for example, with capital punishment, the state supersedes that and says we're still going to kill this person on your behalf. In that instance your personal feeling doesn't matter at all. But when the state wants to justify its vengeance it will say, "We're doing this in the name of the person who was harmed." . . . And we have to govern the world not based on just our personal desires and our personal feelings. We have to have a politic and a set of basic values that we as a society are governed by. Otherwise how are we going to be able to move in the world? We're not going to be able to move in the world if that's not the case and if that's not happening.

It's so complicated. Sometimes our feelings aren't actually aligned with our values. Our expressed value might be, "Well, I don't believe in capital punishment." I may have that value. I don't believe the state has the right to kill in my name, any time ever. And then something happens to a close friend of mine, and my feeling is they should kill this person. We are often at a point where our values don't align with how we feel. In part that's why we're supposed to have a community that can hold when these things are happening so that our feelings don't end up governing how we're going to live in the world, for everybody, how all of us are going to be governed together.

So that may sound convoluted in what I'm talking about right now. I'm thinking as I speak. But also, I've been thinking for a long time about this. In various kinds of ways. And it's a question all the time. People say, "Well, this person was really harmed." And I'll say, "Yes, they were really harmed. Absolutely. And I wish that had not happened. And I also want consequences for that. I just don't think punishment is going to get us there." And I also don't think that using extreme violence to address extreme violence ever works. I think that's just vengeance. I remember watching a terrible Nicole Kidman movie with Sean Penn in it. I even forget the name of the movie. But Nicole Kidman's character at one point says, "Vengeance is a lazy form of grief." And I was like, "Whoa." I had to think about that. It stuck with me. The fact that this thing came out years ago but I still think about it—it really struck a chord in me. Because we need time and space to grieve when hard things happen, when bad things happen to us.

We need that grieving; we need that space. We deserve the support, every part of support, that we can need. Survivors and victims should get multiple supports from the state beyond and not even mainly prosecution. How about paying for people's counseling? How about paying for people to be able to take a trip out of the country so that they can heal or begin the process of figuring out how to heal?

Young: *I'm also really curious to hear more about community accountability. Specifically, how does it work in terms of addressing domestic and sexual violence? These are certainly two areas where it would seem trickier to convince people potentially of a transformative justice approach when the harm we're talking about is such an intimate violation.*

Kaba: Yeah, thanks for asking that question. Actually, the modern aspects of community accountability work are rooted exactly in communities of color, Black, Indigenous, and Latinx people who were overwhelmingly feminists, who started talking about interpersonal harms related to sexual violence and domestic violence. There were obviously folks who were gender nonconforming, trans folks, who were not either able to access the state for "redress" or did not want to access the state, because they knew they might then be criminalized. And in some cases, it was also where people didn't want to access the state. The question was how do we intervene?

The group called INCITE! Women, Gender Nonconforming, and Trans People of Color Against Violence began in the early 2000s to codify things that our communities have been doing to solve issues that arise. To find a way to be present when somebody was harmed. To figure out how to transform the person who caused the harm. This was just a way to codify what many in our communities had been doing for many generations before. There's a wonderful guide created by Mimi Kim, Rachel Herzing, and others, from Creative Interventions, which is like seven hundred pages long. It's online. You can go to CreativeInterventions.com to find it. They just spent several years doing community accountability work in the Bay Area in California, and then took all their lessons that they learned and put it together in this toolkit that they gifted us. That was about fifteen years ago, I think. Ten years ago, at least. They gifted us this resource to use in our communities.

I will always say this too. I think there's something to really be said— and people should be thinking about this more seriously—which is: a lot of people get mad when we talk about community accountability. And they're like, "Well, this doesn't work." And I'm like, "First of all, I don't know what you were doing, but it wasn't community accountability work. It was something else." Often people will use terms with things they didn't understand or don't know how to do and didn't really practice. Or say, "I did a circle with a person." I'm like, "That's not a process. Since when did you talk to a person once and they transformed their entire lives?" It doesn't work that way. Think of yourself. Put yourself in that position and think of how hard it is for you who decided to do something basic like give up sugar, and you cannot stick to it. Because it's hard to do. It's hard to change our behavior. I always think that comes up a lot for people.

Another thing that comes up for people is "You're telling me I have to act in a certain way." I'm not telling you that you have to act any way.

The fact of the matter is that more than 50 percent of people who are harmed, very badly harmed by the way, never contact law enforcement at all in the first place. And so that means they prefer nothing at all, as my friend Danielle Sered says, from Common Justice. They prefer nothing at all rather than what we currently offer. That's a huge number of people who are harmed but don't seek any sort of redress from the state, the thing that is being offered as the end-all, be-all, the only way to transform any harm. So that's already the case.

I'm always like, "Why are you upset? Why are you so invested in being upset with people who are trying something else in order to get the redress that they feel like they need, when more than 50 percent of the people don't even avail themselves of the system that you're fighting so hard to protect and that you're fighting so hard to keep entrenched?" So even of that list of 50 percent that do go in to the system, 50 percent of those folks don't even make it to the point at which there would be a prosecutor sending their case on to petition in the court in any sort of way. They're not even going to grand jury. And then by the time it goes to grand jury, another 50 percent are out. They're not even going to be in a position to be able to go to a trial. And since we know that 98 percent of the people who are in a situation where they might want a trial are actually going to plead out and not go to trial, that's 2 percent of the people in that list who actually go to trial. So, by the time you get to a place where we talk about somebody serving a prison sentence, so many people have not been served by that point that we have got to find a different way to be able to address harm.

As an abolitionist, what I care about are two things: relationships and how we address harm. The reason I'm an abolitionist is because I know that prisons, police, and surveillance cause inordinate harm. If my focus is on ending harm, then I can't be pro deathmaking and harmful institutions. I'm actually trying to eradicate harm, not reproduce it, not reinforce it, not maintain it. We have to realize that sometimes our feelings—and our really valid sense of wanting some form of justice for ourselves—gets in the way of actually seeking the thing we want.

For me, I'm constantly talking with folks. I only facilitate community accountability processes within my communities. I'm not getting paid for it. I'm not a paid facilitator. These things are important. We all have to gain skills within our communities so that we can hold harm, transform it, and come out the other side. That is critical, and so few people are having the harms that they experience attended to at all. Most people get nothing. Community accountability is a way to offer something.

Justice: A Short Story

October 2015

A few years ago, I was invited to contribute to an anthology titled the Feminist Utopia Project. "Justice" is the essay that I submitted for publication. I wanted to think through another world where punishment is not part of the glue that holds a society together. —MK

The ocean is a special kind of blue-green, and I'm standing on the shore watching a woman drown. My friends and family members are witnessing the same scene, or maybe it looks different to their eyes. They are grieving; I am not. I turn to my mother (who is a man) and whisper in his ear: "Vengeance is not justice." And again, "Vengeance is not justice." I let the wind carry my words because human beings (even highly evolved ones) can't hear spirits.

I was sixteen when I died.

Darn, I did it again. I rushed to the end of the story before telling the beginning. I am one of those girls. You know who I mean; the kind of girl who eats dessert for dinner and reads the end of the book first. Everyone calls me impatient. Impatient should be my first name.

I love water and swimming. My father (who claims no gender) says that I must be descended from a fish and not a person. Mama says that he should have named me Aqua. Everyone seems to want to call me by a different name than my actual one, which is Adila, though my friends call me Addie.

I live in Small Place (SP). If someone asked me to describe the sights, sounds, and smells of home, I'd say that SP is very green. I mean you can smell the green and the salt water, and you can hear the wind rustling through the trees. We're family in SP. No, we aren't all related, but we trust and love each other. While arguments and conflicts happen,

157

we always resolve them. My parents are SP's chief peace-holders. If you are wondering how one becomes a chief peace-holder, it's simple really. Anyone over twenty years old is eligible. Every five years a representative group of SP residents gather to consider candidates. Peace-holders are not special or better than anyone else in SP. The only requirements are a desire to serve and a commitment to embody and hold true to our community values. Those values are revisited, reviewed, and sometimes revised annually. Peace-holders' primary responsibilities are to make sure that all of our conflicts are swiftly and peacefully addressed.

Once, I asked Mama why he thought that he was selected as a chief peace-holder. He looked at me for a moment and then said: "I was over twenty years old, willing to serve, and I never forget our common humanity." Mama said that I am good at holding others and myself in our humanity. I'm not sure what he means. I do know that everyone makes mistakes and that we all deserve a chance to be held accountable for them so that we can do and be better next time. Maybe that's like my life philosophy or something. Anyway, what I love the most about living in SP is that we look out for one another; when one person in our community experiences harm, all of us are harmed. It's one of our most sacred and important values.

Though my parents are peace-holders, all of us are circle-keepers. We discuss all of our issues in circle. We celebrate in circle. We mourn in circle. Basically, circles are how we communicate and how we connect. Anyone in our community can call and keep a circle at any time and for any reason. There are no special skills to learn; all you need is to listen and to make space. All ages are included.

I mentioned that we're family in SP. We are a close-knit community, but we often get visitors from other places. Last month, for example, a woman visited SP. She is a distant relative of our neighbors. She came from somewhere called Earth, which is very far indeed. There's nothing memorable about the Earth visitor (EV). Her hair is long and brown. She's pale like she doesn't spend a lot of time in the sun. The only thing that stood out is that she walked around SP carrying a knife in her purse. She said that it was in case "she ran into trouble." She added that on Earth, "women could never be too careful." I didn't understand what she meant. What kind of trouble would you need a knife for? And why would you be in more danger if you identified as a woman? If anything happened, she could just call a circle and together we'd address the issue.

We never locked our doors in SP and our Earth visitor insisted that this was unsafe. "What if someone wants to steal something from the house, or what if they want to hurt someone?" she asked. My mother told her that everything in our house was community property and could be used by anyone. There is no such thing as private property in SP so no one had reason to steal from anyone else when they could simply share what others had. Besides, everyone in SP had their basic needs of food, clothing, and shelter met. Healthcare and education are also freely provided to all members of the community. EV then asked my father if they were afraid for me and my siblings' safety. My father simply shook their head and went to the kitchen to make dinner. Daddy is not the talkative one in our family.

I was so confused by EV's questions that I kept the dictionary tab on my computer open. I looked up words that I didn't understand like "fear" and "stealing." I read the definition of "fear" as "an unpleasant emotion caused by the belief that someone or something is dangerous, likely to cause pain, or a threat." This definition led me to look up more words like "dangerous" and "threat." While I was searching the web, I found a story called a folktale about how people on Earth address conflict and harm. Basically, it goes something like this:

While swimming across a pond, Sis Goose was caught by Brer Fox, who in some versions of the story is a sheriff. A sheriff is a police officer, in case you don't know. I had to look that up too. We have no police in SP. Anyway, Sis gets pissed off because she believes that she has the right to swim in the pond. After all, she's not bothering anyone. She's just minding her own business. So Sis decides to sue Brer Fox. But when the case gets to court, Sis Goose looks around and sees that besides the sheriff who is a fox, the judge is a fox, the prosecuting and defense attorneys are ones too, and even the jury is comprised entirely of foxes. Sis Goose doesn't like her chances. Sure enough at the end of the trial, Sis Goose is convicted and immediately executed. The jury, judge, sheriff, and the attorneys all picked at her bones, which seems even crueler. The moral of the story is: "When all the folks in the courthouse are foxes, and you are just a common goose, there isn't going to be much justice for you."

I worried about this place called Earth and decided that it must be a terrible place to breed such scared, mistrustful, and cruel people. I was glad to be living in SP and resolved to keep my distance from Earth.

At dinner, EV resumed her relentless questioning. She asked where all of the criminals were housed. When we stared blankly, she became agitated and yelled, "The bad people, the bad people, where do you put them?" My mother said that there was no such thing as bad people, only people who sometimes did a bad thing. Our visitor laughed bitterly. "Okay then," she said, "where do you put the people who do bad things?" Finally, I spoke up. "We don't put them anywhere because we all do bad things sometimes and through our relationships with each other we acknowledge the harm we've caused and then we do our best to try to repair it."

EV looked at me like I had grown another head. "You have no prisons here, no jails?"

"No," was our collective response.

Then Mama asked: "How exactly do your prisons and jails address the needs of those who have experienced harm?" EV responded that jails and prisons offered accountability and punishment.

My father asked if punishment was justice and added: "How do those who are locked in your prisons and jails heal? Are they improved by the experience?" That was their word limit for the day, I think.

Our ways and values were alien to EV, and she was clearly disturbed by them. That night, I did some research about the punishment system on Earth and was shocked that the harmed person played almost no role in the process. The trials (I looked up that word too) were the State of Indiana vs. the name of the person who caused harm. Also, it didn't seem like all of the harms were considered "crimes," and some of the "crimes" weren't necessarily very harmful. I read one story of a young girl who was raped, and they actually blamed her for drinking too much at a party. The person responsible for her pain didn't have to acknowledge the harm they caused or make amends. In SP, the entire community would focus first on the needs of the young girl, then we would use circles to discuss what had happened and insist that the person who committed the harm take responsibility. They would be assigned several members of the community to support and guide them in completing the agreed upon restitution. I have to admit, though, that I had a hard time imagining such a thing as rape happening in our community.

One day after school I went for a swim. I got naked and dived into the ocean. I was floating with my eyes closed while thinking about my friend Noliwe, which brought a smile to my face. Noliwe is my most favorite person in SP next to my parents and siblings. I was jolted out of my daydream when I heard someone approach. I opened my eyes and saw that EV was staring at me. She had a knife in her hand.

I was sixteen when I died.

I was killed by a visitor from a place called Earth who couldn't believe that there were no prisons in SP. Mine was the second murder ever in our community, and it fell to my parents as chief peace-holders to ensure that the harm caused was addressed. For days, people across our community convened, communed, celebrated, and consoled each other in circle. There were talking circles, mourning circles, circles of support, and celebration circles. They happened at dawn, in mid-morning, in the evening, and in the dead of night. For days, members of SP told stories about my life through tears, anger, and laughter. There was, however, no talk of punishment or vengeance. Neither would bring me back.

After weeks of centering my family members and friends and of showering them with love, support, and food, the SP community turned its attention to my killer. EV was included in all of the previous circles and so she had experienced the community's outpouring of grief and loss. She heard stories about my life. She knew the extent of the pain felt by my community. After she killed me, she turned herself in to my parents. Her first words to them were: "Where will you put me?"

They responded in unison: "In circle." And so it was that EV came to understand the impact of her actions on an entire community. And so it was that she experienced remorse for her actions and sought to make amends. And so it was that my community held EV in her humanity while seeking to hold her accountable for her actions.

The first murder that occurred in SP happened decades earlier. The ancestors created our Justice Ritual in response. After several days of mourning and celebrating the life of the person killed, the killer's life and actions are explored. In a series of circles, participants discuss why the violence happened, how it happened, and who was harmed. Community members are asked to stand in the shoes of the person who committed the harm, to consider the conditions that underlie their actions, and to examine their own roles in perpetuating those conditions. It was an acknowledgement that no matter how hard we try to purge ourselves of emotions like jealousy, envy, and anger, they remain within us and can negatively impact our relationships. Remaining aware of this is important to maintaining peace.

When circles have been exhausted, the killer is taken to the ocean, tied up, and dropped into the water. This empathy ceremony takes place in front of the entire community. The immediate family members of the victim are given the option of saving the life of the killer or letting them drown. If the family saves the person's life, they are then required to take the place of the person killed within the community. They are expected to pay a debt for the life taken for however long the harmed parties deem necessary, but they do so within the community, living as integrated members.

I saw my father motion to my mother. He nodded his head. EV was rescued from the ocean. When we hold each other in our humanity, what other outcome could there be? Vengeance is not justice.

I was sixteen when I died, and my name was Adila, which means justice.

PART VII

Show Up and Don't Travel Alone: We Need Each Other

"Community Matters. Collectivity Matters."

Interview by Damon Williams and Daniel Kisslinger

Airgo, July 2020

Damon Williams: *How are you treating yourself in this really momentous and high-paced time? And what does that boundary setting look like in terms of maintaining your health? I think we learn a lot of lessons from your boundaries.*

Mariame Kaba: I have been really focused on narrowing in on the things that I think are important and letting go of the rest. I've been enforcing stricter boundaries around what I'll say yes to. So I've said no to many requests that people have made of me, whether it's media requests or whatever. And I've been accepting things that maybe I wouldn't have accepted ten years ago; I'm trying to move myself out of my comfort zone.

Also, I really feel like over the years I've learned myself better. And that helps you to figure out what your actual boundaries are. And also, boundaries are usually a negotiation between what you want and what other people want. It's not like a firm, set thing. You have to get really good at being able to negotiate. And the only way to do that is to know who you are.

Daniel Kisslinger: *Obviously right now in this moment over the last month there are all kinds of new negotiations and boundaries being knocked down and redrawn. What is something that you've seen in the last month or experienced that you didn't think you would ever see?*

Kaba: If I'm 100 percent honest, I don't think there's anything that's happened that I didn't think I would see. I honestly believe that we're going to win the things we fight for. What I'm so encouraged by is the

164

fight. So not that I didn't think I would see it—I never can predict. I'm not Nostradamus. I don't know when protests are going to happen. I don't know when rebellions are going to happen. I don't think anybody does, really.

Kisslinger: *I'm sure that doesn't stop people from asking you when the protest is happening, though.*

Kaba: I don't know when those things are going to happen. I let go of those certainties years ago. My conviction is that we ought to be organizing steadily always. All of the time. When the protests and the uprisings happen we can meet those moments, because we've actually been building all along. Did I think I would see people burning down a police precinct? It's not surprising to me given where we are and given the fact that that particular station was like a horror center for people. For years and years folks on the ground said things are terrible at that third precinct. It makes sense that people would burn that thing down. It's completely rational and logical to me that that would be the case.

Williams: *What I hear from that is we couldn't expect any of this, but it's very easy to accept it. There is no preparing for the organic uprising of people. There's no equation for that. But at some point, that math is going to have to pay off if you keep doing certain things.*

Kaba: I think so. And also, those things aren't independent of continued organizing. These things are dialectical. They influence each other. Spontaneity is real. And happens. Because people take opportunities, situations arise. Sparks happen. Those things are all true. And the thing that can make those moments of real lasting and important change is the ongoing organizing that's been happening all along.

Most people are unaware that this movement has been building for decades, and we have been in this really consistent push and momentum building over the last six years. Now the possibilities feel more real because the media is talking about it. If the news says defund the police and there's a debate about it, now people are engaging it and using their imaginations in completely new ways.

Williams: *Minneapolis used the word* disband *and have voted to disband their police department. In Chicago we are uplifting this fight. And so the* *questions are much more tangible. In addition to this large excitement that I think we'll talk about much more throughout this conversation, there also is this feeling of being naked or being exposed. Because we did not expect 2020 to be the year of uprising and the year where abolition was being talked about on CNN or wherever else. And so now people who think not abstractly or people who think in concrete terms want to know, "Well, then, what do I do tomorrow if you're talking about doing this tomorrow now?" And so, do you feel any of that exposure or any of that nakedness of there are so many things that need to be built with practice? So many things that are going to take lessons and are not going to be immediate, but people now want immediate solutions that we were not six months ago tasked to have?*

Kaba: Yeah. That's a terrific question, honestly. It is a really good question. And I want to say that one of the things that I've learned over the years or that I've cared about most over the years in terms of myself as a PIC abolitionist—I've always been interested in what we're building. That's been a big part of why I do the kinds of things I do and why I built the kinds of containers I've built over the years. It's always interesting to me to think about the *how* of things, the strategy of how we get from where we are to where we want to go. I don't feel extra pressure to give answers right now, but I feel a responsibility to have more people make more things. I've been talking to folks about the importance of us building a million different little experiments, just building and trying and taking risks and understanding we're going to have tons of failure, and failure is actually the norm and a good way for us to learn lessons that help us—

Kisslinger: *Part of the design.*

Kaba: Part of it. The freaking tech folks and the people who are running the banks talk about failure all the time. They normalize that. It's only on the other side of folks who are interested in social transformation and change where failure is not supposed to be a spoken about or a sign that you're horrible or that your ideas don't have merit. I just want us to be building a million different experiments. That's what my energies are focused on in this moment. I read a tweet from someone a couple weeks ago who goes by ZenMarxist on Twitter. They wrote something like, "People want to treat 'we'll figure it out by working to get there' as some sort of rhetorical evasion instead of being a fundamental expression of trust in the power of conscious collective effort." I thought that was so good. We'll figure it out by working to get there. You don't have to know all the answers in order to be able to press for a vision. That's ridiculous. I hope people aren't feeling that kind of pressure, but I do hope people are feeling a sense of wanting to make a bunch of things. I want to try a bunch of things. And maybe the resources will be there this time to actually make that work.

Kisslinger: *And I think so much of the discomfort with that experimentation, the idea of we need a product to sub in for this other product, is this very capitalist mind-set around it, of this is not about process. We hide the process; we hide the labor of it. And then what do we present to the public as our final thing? And the logic of that is in some ways dehumanizing. It's like you should have already had your factory model built for this. No, we're saying stop building factory models where we know what the widget is. Liberation isn't a widget that you can design the pathway toward.*

Kaba: Exactly. Part of the problem with policing, prisons, and surveillance is that it's a one-size-fits-all model. Angela Davis says this perfectly—there is no one alternative. There are a million alternatives. And the issue is to figure out which alternative works for what situation. I don't like to use the word *alternative*, but I will in this case. It's like what works for this particular situation that we're in? What works for these people? How are we going to actually address this based on human needs? These are the things that we're interested in as PIC abolitionists. I think that makes us actually again incredibly creative. Always generative. And also not afraid, again, of failure.

Williams: *Let's stay in that place of this courageous, creative space of generative experimentation. Because you now, in these last however many years, have come into this space, and you get revered, and you also just get limited to the sound bite of making this really horrible system obviously horrible to people. And I know that that is not all that you are. The things that I hear you most passionate about—I don't think people see you as that appropriately. I hear you name yourself as a curator and someone who puts together exhibitions and a librarian of liberatory artifacts and knowledge creation in ways that are not being appreciated. Does that sound accurate?*

Kaba: I don't really care if they're appreciated or not. But I care about them for myself. They're a huge part of who I am. And they're a huge part of how I make sense of the world.

Williams: *I want to borrow that or tap into that I, that curatorial I, because I imagine you have a perspective and are able to see things that at least personally I'll say I'm not seeing. There're these million experiments that are needed, and there're thousands of them that are happening. And it feels like people are taking the steps also to try a whole new load of experiments right now in this time. Are there a few that are in the shadows that excite you or that have challenged you, surprised you, that you've really fallen in love with and want to display on the wall as something that touches your heart as a beautiful human experiment for new solutions?*

Kaba: That's a hard question. Mainly because I don't want to put people on those model trains. What sort of pressure are we putting on the organizations that we say we ought to model ourselves after? Those organizations and groups—and many of them are just formations and collectives—are in no way interested, first of all, in being the model. They're always clear on "We're not the model. We're just trying to figure stuff out in our communities for each other." But also, the pressure of that, then it's like, "Evaluate yourself. Show us the best practice. What is your effectiveness?" The language of neoliberal efficiency models.

Kisslinger: *That sounded just like a project report.*

Kaba: Exactly. And it just destroys whatever creativity and options people had. Most of them aren't even funded groups. They're tiny collectives. I love what Mia Mingus has been doing for years at the Bay Area Transformative Justice Collective where they're working on creating community-based solutions addressing childhood sexual assault and violence. They know that ends up being a fulcrum for people who want to use abolition and discredit it (e.g., "Well, what are you going to do about the child rapists?"). They're very intentionally stepping into that and really doing some powerful work in their communities to build resiliency and safety for children and their families.

I love the models that people are trying out and just testing out right now. The Anti-Terror Police Project in Oakland just launched a community-based mental health response project. They're going to be directly responding to issues that arise in their communities. I love what the folks in LA are trying to do with the Community Action Team 911 (CAT-911) project, which seeds different individual projects at the local level to engage people in alternatives to calling 911.

All these particular things that get my attention focus on the hyper-local. They are really trying to meet the needs of their communities in specific ways, and most of them are completely unfunded or underfunded. That's a problem.

They should be getting a heap of resources in order to be doing their work and taking it to the next level if they want to do that. Those are just a few examples. But then I also look at things that are less hyper-community-level respond-to-harm things that are very much of interest to me. And I think about a lot of projects that people are doing using art, and trying to create new languages to help people understand the moment we're in and what they can do to help support struggle and take action. I'm always just paying attention to what people are trying, and not to be like, "You're the model," but just being like, "What are you doing? I'm so interested in what you're trying to do."

Kisslinger: *If you can't tell, I've been reading your tweets as usual. But there's one other framing that I think has been really helpful for me in this time that I think could be helpful for others also, and it leads right out of that point. We're not just talking about abolishing departments, we're talking about abolishing ideologies and this idea of abolishing policing, and that that process can occur in all kinds of institutions. It can also occur interpersonally and communally. What pieces of that framing do you want to make sure are added into the conversation right now?*

Kaba: I think about that a lot because police are only just a small part—a hugely important part—but just a small part of the larger issue of policing and surveillance that we have to abolish. And I say this all the time quoting my friend Paula Rojas—the cops are in our heads and hearts. Paula was one of the founders of Sista II Sista in Brooklyn years ago. They were running these programs and there would be protests happening and people would run to the cops to get a permit so they can protest. One of her comrades in Chile was like, "Y'all are asking the police for permits to protest the police?" Yeah, the cops are in our heads and hearts, and this is just one small example. But we often reenact cop behavior among each other. We're seeing that in some of the protests. People calling people out and turning them over to the wolves, which are the cops.

There's the question of soft policing, which I don't think is actually soft. It's really rough and hard. People who are coming out of prison are going through reentry, and one of the things they have to do is pee in a cup the social worker gets. They come up dirty with that particular test, and then they're revoked back into the carceral state. This is policing in the form of probation and parole. We understand other forms of "soft policing" that involve the "child welfare protection" system, which is just a law enforcement agency. People think about it as services, but folks from the Movement for Family Power, for example, just put out a new report that helps us to really understand that actually pulling your child away from you is one of the most horrific forms of violence that can be done to a human being. We don't see that as deep policing. And all of those things are super important for us to keep in mind, and to fight as well, alongside. We have to be fighting all these things together . . .

Kisslinger: *Or even if they're not reproducing the police, they're still feeding prisons. So much of people's liberal response as they understand defunding—even in supporting it—is send a social worker. And without an understanding of the ways, like you said, that those institutions are still operating with the same logics and feeding the same structures—*

Kaba: Yes, and part of the carceral state, absolutely . . . I'm thinking a lot about Liat Ben-Moshe who is also in Chicago, and her book called *Decarcerating Disability.* And it's all about the way that everybody is now saying, "Mental health—what we need is a different force that's going to handle mental health." But what are we really saying there? And what are we trying to handle? And what does that look like for the people who are going to be the targets of this? We have to be thinking about the root of all of these kinds of systems and all of these kinds of ideologies and all these visions in order to be able to get to the world we want.

Williams: *I think the relationship you have to this show is not just as some-one who has been on it now three times and someone who is a lovely tweeter and social media advocate of our space, but if people listen diligently, there are so many people who say, I'm using shorthand here, "And then I met Mariame, and then I started to figure these things out." But what they're really saying is, "I entered a space that Mariame Kaba, her colleagues, and this generation of organizers created. This allowed me to shift and transform myself, take new practices, and build bridges with new people."*

You have done this not only in Chicago, and obviously in your home-town in New York City, but also across this county. You are not alone. For me personally and the direct ecosystem of the people that I know—when it was just a dozen of us in this city, little teenagers and twenty somethings screaming at cops, getting beat up, and stressing out, yelling at each other—we had to attribute your work, and what you created that helped us think this way. And now the world is saying these words, saying these ideas. Even if 60 percent of them are getting it wrong when they're saying it, they're trying. They're trying to say these things that were gibberish or a foreign language five years ago, six years ago.

So, on just personal gratitude, here comes my playful accountability. In the formal space, whenever someone speaks or asks me a question about any of this, what I say is, "Don't listen to me. I'm figuring it out and here's what my answer will be. But go and look up any word that Mariame Kaba has said, written, or been a part of." On May 31, I saw tens of thousands of people. And the majority of the signs, the messaging, the energy, was pushing toward abolition and pushing toward defund. I felt so much pride and so much joy and so much confidence, and I felt so affirmed. And I've been doing this for six years. It's not just me.

And in feeling that, I immediately just try to imagine on a human level—outside of her brilliant and humble analysis—how must Mariame really feel right now? I'm imagining twenty or so years of saying this word, saying these ideas, and you have to do it in shadows and have to do it in rooms, and people didn't show up. And groups split apart. All the things and all the labor. But now on a global scale, an uprising that has never been docu-mented before in human history, all over the world, affirming Black life. And the thing that's coming out of this is this new discussion around defunding the police and abolition. Just outside of the dialectics. How did that feel as it really started to set in, like there's something happening right now and I'm a part of making it?

Kaba: Wow. Oh, my goodness. First of all, thank you very much for uplifting the work—as you both know I feel very much that nothing that we do that's worthwhile is done alone. I'm just committed to the notion that everything is collective and collective struggle and collective knowledge. I feel very much like, yes, that makes me happy that that kind of work is being seen by more people. I do want to say—I don't know if you're going to either believe it, or just be like, "What is wrong with her?" But I just haven't felt any sort of "I'm so happy that I've been part of this long-term struggle to get us to this point." I have been very aware, and I'm always happy and excited when people take action. That's just across the board no matter what is going on. I want people to act. And particularly to act in the direction of social change and transformation of the places I want to go.

I'm so elated and I think maybe you noticed that. I'm always a cheerleader for people's actions, including younger people that I've met and known over the years. This is why I uplift all of your work. Meaning you, all of you that I've had the opportunity over the many years to be in rooms with, to be in community with, to be in struggle with. It's because I'm genuinely just so thrilled any time people are taking actions based on a principle and a belief that—what does Ruth Wilson Gilmore say—where life is precious, life is precious. That makes me very excited and happy. And I don't put myself in there. I just never have.

Williams: *Why not?*

Kaba: I grew up and was raised by other organizers to recognize that the self, my self, was not important in the scheme of the larger work that has to happen in order for us to get free. And that while people may want to uplift me separately and put me in a different place, it's my job to always remind everybody of everything else and everybody else.

One of the main reasons I do not ever want to be on screen or in photos is because I always felt like putting me and my face up there was just counterproductive to movement, for multiple kinds of reasons. This is the world that I was engrained to become an organizer in. And it wasn't until I was in my—I would honestly say—my mid-thirties to my late thirties that I started to put my name on anything that I made. For years I never did that. And it was other people who brought it to my attention, particularly a friend of mine who was like, "Interesting, for somebody who is so concerned about history, you seem to write yourself out of it." And it was a moment of accountability for myself, self-accountability, about "What am I telling all these younger people to do and to be?" And then I'm modeling things that may not be useful.

Kisslinger: *It's also not transparent.*

Kaba: Right. It's not transparent. So, yeah, for good or bad, your ideas should be out there for other people to push back on, to add to. To whatever. But they need to know who made some of those things. And made some of those ideas. So, yeah. I don't know if it's a good answer for you, Damon, but it is the answer.

Williams: *It's what I expected. I might challenge a little bit because that is the answer, and I thank you for it because that again is the model and example that we need. I'm very grateful for hearing the intentionality with how you move through space and uplift the collective goal and literally how you embody it. So I'm grateful that you answered in that way. What I'm pulling out is that it is our work, not just the we of Damon and Daniel, but the collective we, to also memorialize and document and name and uplift. That should come outside of you. So it's not that you're blocking it per se or denouncing it. But you are not doing the labor of centering yourself even though it is really historically import-ant that you were centered because we need more young people and people who are not yet here to want to aspire to move through the world the way Mariame Kaba does. So that's the balance that we have to find with you. You got to allow us to do it at least. But I will challenge on this: I hear you on not wanting to take the step or take credit, but on that internal feeling, there were just times of goosebumps. And so maybe not even from a point of accomplishment but just any gratification you saw. Even if you weren't there, just as a documentarian, you saw where this philosophy was twenty years ago.*

Kaba: Yeah. I'm grateful every freaking day. Every day, and that's real. I have a practice of gratitude. I journal every day. And one of the things in my journals is, "What am I grateful for today?" I am consistently living in gratitude. And I also don't like to talk about this publicly because then people think I'm some sort of self-help guru person. That's not what I'm saying. It's deeply a part of my spiritual practice to be grateful for everything. I don't think we're grateful when horrible things happen to us. But we can be grateful for the lessons we learned.

I'm grateful and also, again, super stoked. I'm working with young folks who are organizers in different parts of the country right now on various projects and supporting them in various ways in this moment. I feel so grateful. I'm just like, "How amazing is this that they're working on these things, that they're trying to actualize these ideas?" And that they bothered to ask me for my opinion. That they care, and they're like, "Oh yeah, we really want your help. We want to know how to do this!" Amazing. I'm turning fifty this next year, and I'm like, "That's amazing that folks who are in their early twenties know anything about me and want me to be in the space with them to think through ideas, and to fig-ure out strategy, and to implement a vision. I'm so grateful and so joyful about that. This is less about me and more about a movement that I've been part of for a long time.

One of the first people I ever heard talk about invest/divest was a former political prisoner named Eddie Ellis, who passed away several years ago. Eddie was talking about this in the early 2000s. He was saying we need to divest from punishment and prisons and policing and to invest in our communities. What is it going to take for that to happen? He would go to room after room after room that I was in and would constantly bring up invest/divest. So when I hear folks from the Move-ment for Black Lives in 2014—and 2015—saying invest/divest, I smile because I know that that's Eddie Ellis. And they don't know him, never met him. But he made it possible for us to think that thought, having learned it from somebody else before him.

And maybe you have never heard Eddie Ellis before, and he's also part of this story. He was clear all the time that it's not about him. If you all take this idea and you run with it, I'm going to be so happy from wherever I'm looking down. I believe that, and I believe he's looking down on us right now and smiling every time somebody brings up in-vest/divest and says it's M4BL. Because I don't think he has ego at all in that. He's just going to be like, "Good. These young folks took that shit and ran; I'm so happy."

Kisslinger: *The impact and where the ideas and the lineages show up: that's the whole thing.*

Kaba: That's the whole thing. And the fact that I named his name today means more people know that he had a part in it. But he didn't have to say it.

Kisslinger: *It's not don't have your name known; it's don't make everyone know your name.*

Kaba: Yes.

Kisslinger: *It's a much more gracious and communal way of having your presence in the world. That's very helpful.*

Kaba: Community matters. Collectivity matters. To me that's the whole thing. And if we can't get along with each other, and we can't take responsibility for what we do with each other, then what the hell are we doing? For me, that's the bottom line. If anybody is listening to this who is a young person working in this moment, please be part of the community of folks who are building an accountable community with each other.

Everything Worthwhile
Is Done with Other People

Interview by Eve L. Ewing

Adi Magazine, Fall 2019

It is no surprise that many of those struggling to believe in something in the face of despair have turned to the work of educator and organizer Mariame Kaba. Many (myself included) came to her first through Prison Culture, *the blog she has published since 2010 that explores the many arms of the carceral state and how we might dismantle our current systems of punishment.*

Others may know her from Project NIA, the organization she founded that uses participatory community justice to fight youth incarceration, or one of the many other projects she has founded, cofounded or co-led: campaigns to free Marissa Alexander and Bresha Meadows; the Chicago Freedom School; the Chicago Community Bond Fund; We Charge Genocide; and Reparations Now, which secured reparations for victims of police violence in Chicago.

I spoke with Kaba about her family history, what it means to be an organizer, and the work she's most proud of.

Eve L. Ewing: *Talk to me about coming of age in New York in the 1980s. Your father was also an organizer?*

Mariame Kaba: My dad had been involved in Guinea during the independence struggle. Guinea was the first among the French West African countries to seek independence, and that led to a lot of retribution by the French, sacking our libraries before they left, doing all sorts of stuff.

My father, Moussa Kaba, was then sent to the US by Sékou Touré, who became the first president of the country. They grew up together, and they were friends and comrades in the struggle together. They were all coming up on socialism and Marxism. Touré sent them to study different things so they could come back to build the country after the revolution. My father was going to be a kind of finance minister—that was the notion.

But he started hearing rumors about what was going on postrevolution. Sékou was consolidating power, arresting some of the people who didn't struggle, and locking them up in a prison called Camp Boiro. Camp Boiro became an infamous prison in West Africa, known for disappearing thousands. One of those people that he imprisoned and disappeared is my uncle. When that happened, my father was like, "This is not what we signed up for, and we were not fighting for this consolidation of power and eliminating our comrades who have become enemies because they dissent on one thing."

He decided not to go back. So Sékou's pissed and tells the US to send my father back, to extradite him back to Guinea. The UN heard what was going on, and they gave him a blue passport, a UN passport. This meant that he could renounce his Guinea citizenship to be able to escape having to go back, because Sékou came to the US in a big pompous affair, and he came specifically to get my dad to go back. My father never talked about his life, never talked about this period because of such heartbreak.

Ewing: *Because Sékou was his friend.*

Kaba: They fought together, and he loved him, and they loved each other. This also led many of my family members to move to the Ivory Coast. Everybody, including my grandparents, had to leave because of the political turmoil. My father never got to go back to Guinea until 1986, and that was because Sékou died in 1984. He'd been told that if he set foot in Guinea he'd be arrested.

My father was always avidly interested in politics, and I grew up in a house full of books. And listening to my father's conversations about political struggles around the world—about socialism and its failings, about revolution and what people really mean by "revolution," and what people don't understand about what revolutions really do—this became my political education.

He always told me, "You have a responsibility to live in this world. Your responsibility is not just to yourself. You are connected to everyone." He drilled this into us, to my siblings, "You have each other only. So if you don't get along, you fucking work that shit out because we're not going to be here all the time, and we're not going to be here forever. You have each other." So we are close, close, close, my siblings.

He also said, "You are interconnected to everyone, because the world doesn't work without everyone. You may think that you're alone, but you're never actually alone." This was really important, because that made me understand—at a very young age—the importance of collectivity. We can't do anything alone that's worth it. Everything that is worthwhile is done with other people.

So that became the soundtrack in my head.

My mother was in a different league altogether. She was not political in the same way, but she's incredibly religious and very focused on charity in the sense of mutual aid. My friends were homeless—at the time we lived in the Lower East Side—and I recalled later on how strange it was that my mother just let people stay in our house. But she wasn't going to let those kids stay outside when it was winter.

Ewing: *I see both of those things as such clear strands in your work. On the one hand, organizing collectively and building structures for freedom, resistance, and resilience. And on the other hand, the theme of mutual aid. I wonder as well whether the anticolonial framework, and global Pan-Africanist framework within which your father was working, influences the way you think about politics now.*

Kaba: Always. Always. It made me an internationalist. I can't imagine my organizing not being international and not having an eye toward other people beyond the borders that I live in and also questioning the idea of "borders."

Ewing: *I would venture to say, with my own comparatively short memory, that the languages of repair, reparation, certainly of restorative justice, and also of abolition are moving through discourse in a different way than they have been.*

Kaba: Absolutely.

Ewing: *These are ideas that folks like you have been working on literally since before I was born, that are now being taken up. But what is being* *potentially misunderstood? Where do we need course correction in our conversations there?*

Kaba: That's a really difficult question. Because I'm so uninterested in *narratives*. That word that gets used often. Narrative-building. People that want to be all about narrative-shifting, narrative building.

I believe that when we are in relationship with each other, we influence each other. What matters to me, as the unit of interest, is relationships.

The second thing that matters to me as a unit of impact is harm. I want to figure out how to transform harm in every possible context because I have been harmed, and I have harmed other people. My political commitments are to developing stronger relationships with people and to transforming harm. All those other things you mentioned—the ideas only matter to me to the extent that they impact both those commitments. For example, it is deeply offensive and hurtful to me that we have prisons because they break relationships and people. That's how I feel about prisons—they are inherently made for isolation.

When we talk about repair and restorative justice, it's all about relationships, and relationships in the context of harm. So when people talk about these things as though they are just abstract ideas, or things that are just theory-building without connection to actual people's lives, I can't recognize it.

Ewing: *I think that makes perfect sense because it also is the consequence of what happens when people are learning about concepts primarily through—*

Kaba: Reading.

Ewing: *Right. Like, "I read this interesting article," as opposed to, "I believe in this." Most Black people in Chicago who I know who don't believe in policing, it's not because they read a great article that used debate and rhetoric to convince them but because of their lived empirical experience.*

Kaba: Angela Davis says this perfectly; she's like, knowledge is built through struggle. It isn't just built through somebody theorizing an idea. But through struggle, together, we come up with new concepts and ideas: that's the best thinking.

Ewing: *Do you think it's okay for folks to have different lanes? Where they're like, "I'm just trying to organize for Philly right now," for example. Or do you think that all organizers would benefit from more international experience?*

Kaba: That's a great question. I think we would all benefit from it, just in our political education, but I think it's okay to have your own focus. There's been this struggle over the last few years of people talking about, "I'm just an activist, and I just do things on my own. I don't have anybody who is a base for me, and nobody holds me accountable." And that's not sustainable, and that's also not organizing. That's activism, and activism has its place and is important to do. Most organizers are activists also, but most activists are not organizers, and so we just have to be clear about what we're trying to achieve.

But I do believe lanes are super important, and not all of us care about the same thing. That's also okay. The same passion you feel about saving the whales, somebody else feels about saving pencils. It's not a judgment; we just have different interests.

Ewing: *Let's talk more about organizing and activism because I think that that is a really important distinction. I do not identify as an activist. I am very frequently identified as an activist, which I find very puzzling. What do you see as the difference between those things?*

Kaba: I think that people who are activists are folks who are taking action on particular issues that really move them in some specific way, but activism only demands that you personally take on the issue. That means signing petitions, being on a board of a particular organization that's doing good in the world.

That way, activist is super broad, and that's why people call people activists. Your individual action, for example, of writing can be a form of activism in the sense that it wants to educate people and get them to take action in their own way. You are in that way potentially being activist in your orientation, at least, if not in identity.

Organizers, however, can't exist solo. Because who the hell are you organizing? You can't just decide to wake up one morning and be like, "I'm just going to do this shit." If you're organizing, other people are counting on you, but, more importantly, your actions are accountable to somebody else.

a gut-check moment for me. At least put your name on your shit.

Ewing: *Who are your heroes?*

Kaba: God, I have so many touchstones. I believe in touchstones, people you go back to in particular moments when you need something.

I turn to Baldwin a lot. I read him when I'm feeling a sense of despair over the world that I'm in. I find a sentence that he wrote and it's like, "Ooh, yes."

I think about so many of the Black communist and socialist women of the first part of the century. If they could go through what they went through, if Marvel Cooke could survive the Red Scare and being fired by the *Amsterdam News*—she was the first woman working there ever—if she can endure that in the 1930s, what am I doing? You know what I mean? Now I have so much more at my disposal. I'm so much less oppressed.

I love Ida B. Wells-Barnett. I love reading her journal where she's lamenting that she can't stop spending money, like, "Why did I buy that scarf? My God. Why am I spending this money?" And it's beautiful, because it shows you this woman who fearlessly went to the South by herself to literally take down people's testimony after a lynching, just sitting around saying, "Why can't I fucking stop shopping? Why did I buy this super expensive scarf that I cannot afford?" It makes me so happy to go back to that and read that passage and be like, "Yes, Ida!"

Ewing: *And to reclaim the humanity of Black women also, you know? There's one part in her autobiography where she's like, "I think I was the first person to do a speaking tour while nursing a baby." Sometimes her baby cried in the middle of her thing, and she was embarrassed, and she had to go out.*

Kaba: That image of her going to that meeting, and Harriet Tubman was there, and Ida giving her son to Harriet Tubman, and Harriet Tubman raising the son and calling him the movement's baby? Oh my God. I love that shit.

Angela Davis is a huge touchstone for me. Ruthie Wilson Gilmore is a touchstone for me. Beth Richie is a touchstone for me. A lot of Black feminist women who I've been able to be in space with in real life. Some who've given me a way of being in the world. Modeling grace in moments that are really not graceful.

Camara Laye is a beautiful Guinean writer who I love reading. Also, Walt Whitman; I love his poetry. I will read and get influences from everyone.

Ewing: *What questions are plaguing you right now?*

Kaba: How are we going to organize ourselves in this protofascist moment in the US and around the world? The *how* of it is what I'm stuck on. I'm not stuck on the capacity of us to do it.

Ewing: *Do you believe we can do it?*

Kaba: Not only do I believe it, I know we can. Because people have. People lived through the '20s and '30s. A lot of people died, but a lot of people lived, and people fought. It did take war. I think about war a lot. I think about it in the context of abolition, knowing full well that there could not have not been the abolition of slavery without the Civil War.

Frederick Douglass—everybody thought he was a militant psychopath because he kept saying, "The war had to come. We're going to have to go to war. That's the only way we're going to be able to get out of this." And people, including Black people, saying, "No, no, no," and "Stop using this term," and" We don't want to go to war," and him saying, "That's the only way."

Ewing: *"That's dangerous."*

Kaba: Many said he was literally harming us with that talk. "We are in a position where they're going to come and shoot all of us down, and you're fucking out here making these speeches about war." What he must have had to sit with in that moment of time, when it was unclear whether there would be one, and still say, "It must happen," and then six hundred thousand deaths later. . . . Right? To sit in that.

Ewing: *A war that our country is not over. Not remotely over.*

Kaba: Not even close to being over. So I'm thinking a lot about how we're going to organize ourselves in this moment, in our oppressive protofascist moment, and I'm thinking about if we're going to need war again in order to actually facilitate the next phase of the long abolitionist phase. Kind of the Third Reconstruction that some people are talking about.

Then, I'm thinking a lot about Blackness in the twenty-first century. Because there are Native people, Indigenous people the world over, having survived eliminationist policies, having survived genocide ... where are we in relationship to them? We need deep solidarity and co-struggleship with folks. But while we need that more than ever, we're in a conversation right now over land trust around reparations in the United States and other parts of the world, when we are not on our land. There were people here.

Ewing: *Right. I don't know how we're going to work that out.*

Kaba: We work it out by permission. The very things we're talking about doing in restorative justice and repair. We have to internalize those values within our conversations with people. I'm okay with having conversations about Black people who landed in the United States, for people whose ancestors were enslaved toiling on this land, coming here without choice, being brought here, but your work is still permission-driven, because there were people here, even though you came against your will. There were people here already. So what do you owe to that and to them?

Ewing: *The problem with that is it requires relationships, right?*

Kaba: This is the point, and we don't have any.

Ewing: *Well, now I feel like I have to end on some sort of positive note. But I don't. I guess no one is going to open the Eve Ewing/Mariame Kaba interview and be like, "I'm ready to feel great. I'm ready to feel good."*

Kaba: People should. You know why?

Ewing: *Why?*

Kaba: I'm going to tell you why. The reason I'm struggling through all of this is because I'm a deeply, profoundly hopeful person. Because I know that human beings, with all of our foibles and all the things that are failing, have the capacity to do amazingly beautiful things too. That gives me the hope to feel like we will, when necessary, do what we need to do.

But one of the important things is identifying where the issues are—and I don't think hiding from that and pretending like everything is possible, everything is good—but to be rigorous and to be clear-eyed. "This is fucked up, and what can we be doing?" It's not the individuals. I would be very depressed if it only was up to me to solve every problem in the world, but it's not. Or you.

I look at the evidence, and I see the fucked-up-ness of it. But I always look to the possibilities that exist, still, for us to have more freedom, to get toward that horizon we're all trying to work for.

Resisting Police Violence against Black Women and Women of Color

Remarks at "Invisible No More: Resisting Police Violence
against Black Women and Women of Color in Troubled Times,"
Barnard College, New York, November 2017

When I heard that Barbara Smith was going to be on the panel I remembered that one of the first examples of a defense campaign that the Combahee River Collective was involved with in Boston (after Joan Little), was the case of a woman named Ella Mae Ellison. This was a wrongful conviction case that Combahee and people in Boston organized around to free a woman who'd been wrongfully convicted on a first-degree murder charge and a conspiracy to commit armed robbery charge.

We learned something about how to do campaigns around freeing women who were criminalized by the state wrongly from that experience. So I have a lot of gratitude to all of you for that work and for paving the way forward for the rest of us to learn and be able to keep pushing. Thank you so much for that. Of course, Kim Crenshaw's work has helped us to center on the burdens placed on people based on their social locations, which create new suffering. And that's been something that's been important. And I went to college in Montreal and Robin Maynard is from Montreal. I do know that slavery existed in Canada. They taught us that much at McGill. So I'm really grateful for her work and focus on Canada and bringing in the anti-Blackness history of that. So that also informs me.

I was thinking about how I came to this work just the other day. I grew up in New York City, and I went to my first anti–police brutality demonstration when I was fourteen years old, right here in New York. So I've been doing work for a long time around these issues. Even before I understood that I was doing work around these issues! And I've engaged in multiple contexts. Eleanor Bumpers was killed when I was thirteen years old. And the person who killed her was acquitted when I was fifteen. I remember very clearly that she was killed. I remember that people were organizing against her killing. I don't remember organizing against it, because I thought very much that the killing of Black men was the main thing we were fighting to end. I didn't see myself so much as a woman or a girl. In terms of my own identity, my gender didn't figure in the way that my race did.

Also, I grew up in Black nationalist organizing. And this just was a different conversation. It wasn't until I was older that I gained an understanding of myself as a gendered person and that I claimed woman as an identity for myself that would also be part of my organizing. So I think that's the case for many of us who started doing work around anti–state violence work, particularly in the 1980s. That seemed to be the case for a lot of my peers at least.

I also wanted to say how I came into the work was mainly actually through doing political prisoner defense campaigns. And particularly the MOVE Nine, Ramona Africa, and all the women who were either killed or were imprisoned, some of whom are still in prison today, over a mass terroristic police attack against Black people in the United States. Something that does not get talked about as a form of police violence. But it's the ultimate form of state violence—throwing bombs on a bunch of people in their homes.

That really was a radicalizing event for me. And it helped me to start to think about state violence in a different way. It involved including new people and new harms, and it forced me to widen my lens. To look at lethal force not as just one form of violence perpetrated against people on a daily level. If we add up the numbers of people killed versus the number of people sexually assaulted, harassed, harmed, wrongfully convicted, many more people are impacted.

When we itemize atrocities, we often think about the deaths over everything else. This is a problem. Because everything else is what's with us, the living. So I think a lot about the word *accumulation*. It means to gather and pile up especially little by little. That's what's happening with police killings. But accumulation does not enumerate harm. What we have is actually an excess of harm, and this excess can't be measured. When this happens, I think we can find ourselves at a loss in our discussion and in our actions, in part because our definitions are so wanting of what is actually happening.

What happens when you define policing as actually an entire system of harassment, violence, and surveillance that keeps oppressive gender and racial hierarchies in place? When that's your definition of policing, then your whole entire frame shifts. And it also forces you to stop talking about it as though it's an issue of individuals, forces you to focus on the systemic structural issues that need to be addressed in order for this to happen.

It also gives us space to consider other kinds of victims. And other kinds of harms that are foreclosed when we use terms like *police brutality* and *violence*. This is not an issue of *police brutality*. And police violence is a misnomer. It's actually redundant because policing is violence. In and of itself. It is.

So I guess I just want to put out there that we are in deep trouble. And we're in deep trouble because we're not talking about the same things. And when you start talking about policing as a system that's actually about harassment, violence, and surveillance, then you're not going to accept bullshit reform. You're going to understand from the beginning that what we're talking about is the horizon of abolition. It's the only way. So I just want to put that out there.

Join the Abolitionist Movement

Interview by Rebel Steps

Liz: *Abolition has been a huge topic in the wake of the uprising sparked by the police murders of George Floyd and Breonna Taylor. Calls to defund or abolish the police are now experiencing a surge. As soon as "defund the police" emerged as a widespread demand, centrist organizations and elected officials quickly moved to redirect the movement. There are also attempts to redefine the demands. . . . And there's just everyday people that are learning about this for the first time and trying to understand it in the midst of these attempts to moderate the demands.*

Mariame Kaba: I think that some of what's happening isn't so much co-optation. Rather, I think that people are new to these ideas. They're trying to make sense of it in real time, and they're projecting the meanings that they want and need onto these ideas. I want us to be generous with ourselves and understanding with others. Oftentimes when you encounter something for the first time, it raises so much within you, it makes you grasp for familiar things to explain the thing that you may not quite understand.

I do agree that there are kind of malevolent forces that are purposely twisting ideas and trying to fix those ideas to fit within what they already want to do. But that's mostly people with power and the elites. They're always working toward that goal, and some reformers are the middle management for the elite, and they're trying to do the same thing. But if you're new to the movement, you're trying to understand what PIC abolition is, you're trying to avoid co-optation of it.

It's good to know that abolition is a flexible praxis, contingent on social conditions and communal needs, but it's built on a set of core principles. And you declare yourself to be an abolitionist, a PIC abolitionist, then you're making some basic commitments. They include the understanding that prison-industrial complex abolition calls for the elimination of policing, imprisonment, and surveillance. That PIC abolition rejects the expansion and legitimation of all aspects of the PIC, including surveillance and policing and imprisonment of all sorts. And PIC abolition really refuses premature death and organized abandonment, as Ruth Wilson Gilmore talks about. Both premature death and organized abandonment are the state's modes of reprisal and punishment. These principles matter.

And you have to know that you can advocate for radical reform of surveillance and policing and sentencing and imprisonment without defining yourself as a PIC abolitionist. This may need to be explicitly stated in this current historical moment for folks; part of how we prevent co-optation is that we have to let people know that everyone doesn't have to be an abolitionist. We must hold the line on these core commitments and obligations. We really push back by consistently always stating those core principles. If you don't want the elimination of policing, imprisonment, and surveillance, then you're not a PIC abolitionist.

Liz: *As new people look for ways to join movements, it's inevitable that some will search for a quick fix. If you're new and looking to get involved, remember that it's not about just hashtags or a day of protest. It's about joining the struggle.*

Kaba: That's in the air, right? On the question of allies, I've mentioned that I don't believe in allyship, and I'm super bored with the concept of performativity. I believe in strugglers and I believe in coworkers and I believe in solidarity. I believe we need more people all the time in all of our work, in all of our movements, in all of our struggles. The question is how do we get folks to struggle alongside us and with us. As an organizer, this is the constant thinking I am engaged in. What are points of entry for people, so that they can find a way to lend what they know how to do, their talent, their ideas to whatever it is that we're doing, while also learning in the process?

I think about sites of struggle as just constant learning. I'm an incredibly curious person, and I feel like that's a huge help in my work.

It's helpful to be super curious, come with what you know, be willing to learn, and to be willing to be transformed in the service of the work. Mary Hooks has that right—that you have to be willing to be transformed in the service of the work and the struggle. And if you're coming to things in that way, then you know you'll be welcome. If you're not welcome, then you'll make a place for yourself where you can be welcome.

"I Must Become a Menace to My Enemies": The Living Legacy of June Jordan

Remarks at "The Difficult Miracle: The Living Legacy of June Jordan," Cambridge, Massachusetts, February 2018

People often get up on these occasions and say that it's really an honor to be in the space with everyone here, and they usually will then thank the organizers of the event for their hard work, and then they'll say that they're really thrilled to be sharing the stage with such illustrious co-panelists, whom they greatly admire, and then they'll say that they want to take a moment to actually thank the audience for showing up in a terrible snowstorm that's about to start, and I know you all want to get home as soon as possible.

And that's what people usually say at times like these, and these are things that are true for me, today.

But also, for me, WTF, I cannot believe that I was invited to speak at an event commemorating the legacy of June Jordan! June Jordan, who has been a touchstone of mine, really, since I first read her work in college, which was many, many years ago. So I really can't believe that I'm here today, and I'm really grateful to be here with all of you to celebrate her legacy and her life.

June Jordan loved Black people, and so do I. She was an educator, and so am I. She was an activist; so am I. She was an internationalist, and so am I. She was a brilliant writer, and I am not—at all. So bear with me.

Before I was anything though, I was a youth worker and I was this when I was fifteen, and I am still at forty-six. Youth workers teach, we mentor, we advocate, we counsel, we consult. Most of all, we love. We love young people. When I read Jordan's essay, "Nobody Mean More to Me Than You and The Future Life of Willie Jordan," the youth worker in

193

me recognized myself in the now hundreds of young people I've taught, counseled, and loved over the past decades.

So this brings me to Michael, to the future life of Michael. "Michael's been shot," the voice on the phone says, "He's alive, he'll recover." I breathe easier, temporarily relieved. It's a reprieve. Michael is eighteen, and he's on borrowed time. He reminds me regularly that he's not long for this world. I've heard the words (in some variation) so often that they now pour off me like water from the shower head. What is the antidote to the certainty about one's impending death? How does one live with the specter of death as a constant companion? The certainty is a thief. It robs me of language. I've lost my tongue.

I want to break my silence to say that I love him, and I would be devastated if he didn't live until he's at least one hundred, but I don't respond. I pretend that I don't hear the words. I'm numb, and after all, I can't guarantee that he will live to become an old man. He's young, he's Black, he's poor, he lives on the West Side of Chicago. I steel myself for bad news every morning and this time it arrives.

Michael belongs to the tribe of the young and the unmoored. His body is passing through, and he has no expectations of staying. We rode on the 'L' train together once. Michael's voice boomed throughout the trip. I asked him to lower it. He looked at me for a moment and kept loud talking. I was embarrassed at his display, and I felt disrespected that he ignored my request. These are emotions that youth workers feel. As soon as we got off the 'L,' his voice returned to its normal decibel level. I asked why he spoke so loudly on the train. His response: "I want them uncomfortable and they need to know that I was here." My anger dissipated. I've never forgotten his words. They're seared in my mind. "They need to know that I was here." Michael and I had never spoken of what it's like to feel not here.

In Michael's words, I hear June Jordan's, "I will no longer lightly walk behind a one of you who fear me: Be afraid. I plan to give you reasons for your jumpy fits and facial tics. I will not walk politely on the pavements anymore. I must become, I must become a menace to my enemies."

Michael is in fact a menace to society: a problem to be managed, controlled, and contained by any means necessary. He knows it and is expected to swallow his rage as he is surveilled in stores and on the streets, as he is targeted by cops for endless stops and frisks, as he's repeatedly denied jobs, as his schools are closed, as he looks over his shoulder, dodging bullets, and as he is locked in cages with thousands who look just like him.

A young man who has been behind bars for most of his formative years has told me on more than one occasion that he was always certain his life held only two viable possibilities: "die in the streets or die in prison." Jordan tells us, "Most Americans have imagined that problems affecting Black life follow from pathogenic attributes of Black people and not from the malfunctions of the state." I've been a witness to the malfunctions of every Chicago institution (schools, government, law enforcement, and more), malfunctions that pile up and crush hope. Poet and teacher Kevin Coval has written, "Every institution in Chicago fails Black youth. Segregated and systematically inequitable, Chicago is a town where white kids exist in an increasingly idyllic new urban utopia, and Black and Latino kids weave and dodge through a war zone."

Michael has been in and out of confinement since he was thirteen. My work has meant being a witness to the everyday damage that incarceration does to the future prospects of so many people who get caught in systems of arrest, jail, surveillance, and rearrest. This cycle makes it harder for individuals to find and hold onto stable housing, jobs, and relationships. It aggravates mental health and substance abuse problems. Prisons are not places for transformation, and they are not appropriate social service providers. Incarceration is a traumatic experience. People spend years after their release working to heal. Michael is unhealed, still.

I visit Michael in the hospital, and I hate hospitals. He smiles wanly. I burst into tears. The temporary relief I feel is quickly replaced by dread that can't be dislodged from the pit of my stomach. I worry about retaliation. I worry that violence begets more violence. I worry about Michael. This is a young man living in exile in his own country, where his humanity is unacknowledged. He languishes in a place that Richard Wright has called "No Man's Land," or maybe it's the place June Jordan called "otherwhere." He is allowed no feelings. He is just a threat: all of our fears rest on and in him.

I remember our ride on the 'L' and his words to me, "They need to know that I was here," and I recognize that he is demanding to be seen in all of his humanity by the larger world. Yet one constant throughout American history is a persistent denial of Black humanity, and the callous disregard of Black pain. June Jordan understood this all too well, but she was not defeated by it. She insisted that by organizing, we have the power to overcome oppression. I too believe this to be true. She was righteously outraged; I am too. As far as I know, Michael hasn't taken part in the ongoing Movement for Black Lives protests and organizing. His struggle is to live day to day. His resistance is to stay alive, and he is courageous in his personal fight.

June talked a lot about courage. The courage of South Africans fighting against Apartheid and of students sitting in to insist that Columbia and Harvard divest from it. She reminded us of "the truth that only evil will collaborate with evil." Were she alive today, I believe that she'd tell us that the prison industrial complex is evil, and we must not collaborate. We must refuse. For me, that refusal is rooted in an abolitionist politic. As Morgan Bassichis, Alexander Lee, and Dean Spade write, "We see the abolition of policing, prisons, jails and detention not strictly as a narrow answer to 'imprisonment' and the abuses that occur within prisons, but also as a challenge to the rule of poverty, violence, racism, alienation, and disconnection that we face every day. . . . Abolition is the practice of transformation in the here and now and the ever after."*

I've organized for many years alongside young people, so I am of course inspired by the high school students who are currently in the streets, demanding a change to gun laws and saying that they refuse to be used for target practice. But their activism is not new. We've seen young people of color—particularly young Black and brown people—facing down tanks, demanding policy change, and insisting that Black lives matter for five years now. And we've seen their forebears do the same for fifteen and one hundred years before.

The Dream Defenders descended on Tallahassee, Florida, to occupy the capitol when Trayvon Martin was killed almost six years ago next Monday. They demanded an end to racist Stand Your Ground gun laws then. We like to forget, to un-see what has already happened in this country, particularly if the people we need to remember and see are of color, or LGBTQ, or poor, or undocumented, or Muslim, or, or, or.

---

* Morgan Bassichis, Alexander Lee, Dean Spade, "Building an Abolitionist Trans and Queer Movement with Everything We've Got," in *Captive Genders: Trans Embodiment and the Prison Industrial Complex*, expanded 2nd ed., eds. Eric A. Stanley and Nat Smith (Oakland, CA: AK Press, 2015), 42–43.

Sonia Sanchez encourages us to "call on our residual memories." She reminds us that in political struggle, we must call on our ancestors who can help us to navigate our present-day trials. She is speaking about the importance of spirituality, in whatever form it might manifest for you. "We must hear the voices and have the dreams of those who came before us, and we must keep them with us in a very real sense. This will keep us centered." Aren't we blessed that June Jordan is one of the ancestors who we can call on and hear her voice to keep us centered in this current stormy weather?

What can we hear from her in this moment? I think that love is a requirement of principled struggle, both self-love and love of others, that we must all do what we can, that it is better to do something rather than nothing, that we have to trust others as well as ourselves. I often repeat the adage that "hope is a discipline." We must practice it daily. June's work teaches us this truth.

In "Tonight it is my privilege to stand with you," a poem written on September 11, 2001, Jordan tells us about "resolving to work harder than I have ever worked for the sake of justice, which is the only true path to peace." This is written several months before she dies in 2002.

I'm calling on all of us to do the same, to secure the future lives of all of the Michaels and the Michelles in our country and beyond.

Acknowledgments

Many years ago, I adopted a gratitude practice. Every day, I write at least two things that I'm grateful for in my journal. This book would not be possible without the support, collaboration, and partnership of many people. While I can't list everyone, I want to at least express my gratitude for a few.

I'm grateful to write and think with friends and comrades like Shira Hassan, Kelly Hayes, Rachel Herzing, Erica Meiners, Tamara Nopper, Andrea Ritchie, and Red Schulte. Thank you to everyone who has invited me to share my ideas in interviews and presentations and talks over the years. Thanks to all of the people who I've been blessed to organize with and alongside for the past few decades.

I'm grateful to my family for their love and support that make so much possible in my life. Finally, special thanks to the dream team that brought this book into being: Julie, Rachel, Naomi, and Tamara.

Sources and Permissions

Part I: So You're Thinking about Becoming an Abolitionist

- "So You're Thinking about Becoming an Abolitionist," orignially titled "Abolition for the People: So You're Thinking about Becoming an Abolitionist," by Mariame Kaba, reprinted with permission of Kaepernick Publishing and *LEVEL*, October 30, 2020.

- "The System Isn't Broken," originally titled "Summer Heat," by Mariame Kaba, reprinted with permission of *The New Inquiry*, June 8, 2015.

- "Yes, We Mean Literally Abolish the Police," by Mariame Kaba, reprinted with permission of *The New York Times*, June 12, 2020.

- "A Jailbreak of the Imagination: Seeing Prisons for What They Are and Demanding Transformation," by Mariame Kaba and Kelly Hayes, reprinted with permission of *Truthout*, May 3, 2018.

- "Hope Is a Discipline," reprinted with permission of *Beyond Prisons* podcast, January 5, 2018.

Part II: There Are No Perfect Victims

- "Free Marissa and All Black People," by Mariame Kaba, reprinted with permission of *In These Times*, November 26, 2014.

- "Not a Cardboard Cutout: Cyntoia Brown and the Framing of a Victim," by Mariame Kaba and Brit Schulte, reprinted with permission of *The Appeal*, December 6, 2017.

- "From 'Me Too' to 'All of Us': Organizing to End Sexual Violence without Prisons," interview with Mariame Kaba and Shira Hassan by Sarah Jaffe, reprinted with permission of *In These Times*, January 15, 2018.

- "Black Women Punished for Self-Defense Must Be Freed from Their Cages," by Mariame Kaba, reprinted with permission of *The Guardian*, January 3, 2019.

Part III: The State Can't Give Us Transformative Justice

- "Whether Darren Wilson Is Indicted or Not, the Entire System Is Guilty," by Mariame Kaba, reprinted with permission of *In These Times*, November 17, 2014.

- "The Sentencing of Larry Nassar Was Not 'Transformative Justice.' Here's Why," by Mariame Kaba and Kelly Hayes, reprinted with permission of *The Appeal*, February 5, 2018.

- "We Want More Justice for Breonna Taylor than the System That Killed Her Can Deliver," by Mariame Kaba and Andrea J. Ritchie, reprinted with permission of *Essence* magazine, July 16, 2020.

Part IV: Making Demands: Reforms for and against Abolition

- "Police 'Reforms' You Should Always Oppose," by Mariame Kaba, reprinted with permission of *Truthout*, December 7, 2014.

- "A People's History of Prisons in the United States," interview with Mariame Kaba by Jeremy Scahill, reprinted with permission of *Intercepted* podcast, May 31, 2017.

- "Arresting the Carceral State," by Mariame Kaba and Erica R. Meiners, reprinted with permission of *Jacobin*, February 24, 2014.

- "Itemizing Atrocity," by Tamara K. Nopper and Mariame Kaba, reprintd with permission of *Jacobin*, August 15, 2014.

- "'I Live in a Place Where Everybody Watches You Everywhere You Go,'" drawn from remarks at the Forty-Third Annual Scholar and Feminist Conference, "Subverting Surveillance: Strategies to End State Violence" at Barnard College, February 2018.

- "Toward the Horizon of Abolition," interview with Mariame Kaba by John Duda, reprinted with permission of *Next System Project,* November 9, 2017.

Part V: We Must Practice and Experiment: Abolitionist Organizing and Theory

- "Police Torture, Reparations, and Lessons in Struggle and Justice from Chicago," combines the essay originally titled "'We Must Love Each Other': Lessons in Struggle and Justice in Chicago," by Mariame Kaba, reprinted with permission of *Prison Culture* blog, February 15, 2015 and the essay originally titled "Police Torture, Reparations, and Echoes from the 'House of Screams,'" by Mariame Kaba, reprinted with permission of *Prison Culture* blog, May 7, 2015.

- "Free Us All: Participatory Defense Campaigns as Abolitionist Organizing," by Mariame Kaba, reprinted with permission of *The New Inquiry,* May 8, 2017.

- "Rekia Boyd and #FireDanteServin: An Abolitionist Campaign in Chicago" combines "On Showing Up, Erasing Myself, and Lifting Up the Choir . . . ," by Mariame Kaba, reprinted with permission of *Prison Culture* blog, April 28, 2015; "#FireDanteServin: An Abolitionist Campaign in Chicago," by Mariame Kaba, reprinted with permission of *Prison Culture* blog, September 19, 2015; and "Four Years since a Chicago Police Officer Killed Rekia Boyd, Justice Still Hasn't Been Served," by Mariame Kaba, reprinted with permission of *In These Times,* March 21, 2016.

- "A Love Letter to the #NoCopAcademy Organizers from Those of Us on the Freedom Side," by Mariame Kaba, reprinted with permission of *Prison Culture* blog, March 13, 2019.

Part VI: Accountability Is Not Punishment: Transforming How We Deal With Harm and Violence

- "The Practices We Need: #MeToo and Transformative Justice," interview with Mariame Kaba, reprinted with permission of *How to Survive the End of the World* podcast, November 7, 2018.

- "Moving Past Punishment," interview with Mariame Kaba, reprinted with permission of *For the Wild* podcast, December 27, 2019.

- "Justice: A Short Story," by Mariame Kaba, reprinted with permission of Alexandra Brodsky and Rachel Kauder Nalebuff, eds., *The Feminist Utopia Project* (New York: Feminist Press, 2015).

Part VII: Show Up and Don't Travel Alone: We Need Each Other

- "Community Matters. Collectivity Matters," originally titled "The Abolition Suite Vol. 2," interview with Mariame Kaba, reprinted with permission of *AirGo* podcast, July 1, 2020.

- "Everything Worthwhile Is Done with Other People," interview with Mariame Kaba by Eve L. Ewing, reprinted with permission of *Adi Magazine*, Fall 2019.

- "Resisting Police Violence against Black Women and Women of Color" drawn from remarks at "Invisible No More: Resisting Police Violence Against Black Women and Women of Color in Troubled Times," in New York along with Barbara Smith, Kimberlé Crenshaw, and Reina Gossett, sponsored by the Barnard Center for Research on Women, November 2017.

- "Join the Abolitionist Movement," interview with Mariame Kaba, reprinted with permission of *Rebel Steps* podcast.

- "I Must Become a Menace to My Enemies," drawn from remarks at "The Difficult Miracle: The Living Legacy of June Jordan" in Cambridge, Massachusetts, along with Imani Perry and Solmaz Sharif, sponsored by the Radcliffe Institute for Advanced Study, February 28, 2018.

Index

"Passim" (literally "scattered") indicates intermittent discussion of a topic over a cluster of pages.

About Haymarket Books

Haymarket Books is a radical, independent, nonprofit book publisher based in Chicago. Our mission is to publish books that contribute to struggles for social and economic justice. We strive to make our books a vibrant and organic part of social movements and the education and development of a critical, engaged, international left.

We take inspiration and courage from our namesakes, the Haymarket martyrs, who gave their lives fighting for a better world. Their 1886 struggle for the eight-hour day—which gave us May Day, the international workers' holiday—reminds workers around the world that ordinary people can organize and struggle for their own liberation. These struggles continue today across the globe—struggles against oppression, exploitation, poverty, and war.

Since our founding in 2001, Haymarket Books has published more than five hundred titles. Radically independent, we seek to drive a wedge into the risk-averse world of corporate book publishing. Our authors include Noam Chomsky, Arundhati Roy, Rebecca Solnit, Angela Y. Davis, Howard Zinn, Amy Goodman, Wallace Shawn, Mike Davis, Winona LaDuke, Ilan Pappé, Richard Wolff, Dave Zirin, Keeanga-Yamahtta Taylor, Nick Turse, Dahr Jamail, David Barsamian, Elizabeth Laird, Amira Hass, Mark Steel, Avi Lewis, Naomi Klein, and Neil Davidson. We are also the trade publishers of the acclaimed Historical Materialism Book Series and of Dispatch Books.

Also Available from Haymarket Books

1919
Eve L. Ewing

Border and Rule
Global Migration, Capitalism, and the Rise of Racist Nationalism
Harsha Walia, afterword by Nick Estes, foreword by Robin D.G. Kelley

Electric Arches
Eve L. Ewing

Freedom Is a Constant Struggle
Ferguson, Palestine, and the Foundations of a Movement
Angela Y. Davis, edited by Frank Barat, preface by Cornel West

From #BlackLivesMatter to Black Liberation
Keeanga-Yamahtta Taylor

How We Get Free
Black Feminism and the Combahee River Collective
Edited by Keeanga-Yamahtta Taylor

Missing Daddy
Mariame Kaba, illustrated by bria royal

#SayHerName: Black Women's Stories of State Violence and Public Silence
African American Policy Forum, edited by Kimberlé Crenshaw
Foreword by Janelle Monáe

We Still Here: Pandemic, Policing, Protest, and Possibility
Marc Lamont Hill, edited by Frank Barat
Foreword by Keeanga-Yamahtta Taylor

"When the Welfare People Come"
Race and Class in the US Child Protection System
Don Lash